Elaine Trimlett Glover was born in Leicester, United Kingdom, in the 1960s. Influenced by her teachers, Mr Page and Geoff Parker, at Stonehill and Longslade school, English literature was her favourite subject. Elaine has many talents—journalism, writing and a love for adventure. In the early 1980s, Elaine lived in Belfast and was married to an RUC Officer, then after returning to England she became an antique dealer and furniture restorer. In 2005, she became a carer to her husband, Nigel, who passed away in 2010. Elaine left for Southampton and having a strong faith in Jesus she became a missionary in Baghdad, Iraq, and rural Kenya where she was responsible for infrastructure and girls' education. In 2015, returning to UK, she almost died of Cerebral Malaria but she survived through prayer and faith in God. Married Adrian in Christchurch, Jerusalem, by Canon Andrew White on Passover and a Presenter of a local Christian Radio Station in Bournemouth and Presenter in a Community Radio in Swanage.

She is also a Bishop of the Cross Denominational Mission plus Bishop of Makongeni Church, Kenya.

I would like to dedicate *Don't Take Care, Take Risks* firstly to my dear friend, Raouf Rashid Abd al-Rahman, the Chief Judge who sentenced Saddam Hussein, and his beautiful Kurdish family. Secondly, to my dear friend Canon Andrew White, for all his work in the Middle East with reconciliation, diplomacy, as a hostage negotiator and as the Archbishop's Envoy. Also, for his great work with Jerusalem Merit—founded in 2018, supports the Iraqi Refugee community in Jordan, by relieving poverty and financial hardship.

Also, I would like to dedicate this book to Brian Fuche, 'Brian the Squirrel', for his tireless work with the Kurdish people in Portsmouth and Erbil, especially with his work at the 'Hiwa' Hope Community Centre, for Kurds. Portsmouth' Brian was responsible for the Halabja, in Southsea, Portsmouth, and is a Trustee for Jerusalem Merit, and has also been to visit the Raouf family many times.

Not forgetting Judith Kirby for her wonderful work with the Kurdish women in Portsmouth and I would also like to dedicate the book to Esther Lombardi from Hollywood, USA, for her ministry to help the Kurdish people.

Elaine Trimlett Glover

Don't Take Care, Take Risks

AUSTIN MACAULEY PUBLISHERS™
LONDON • CAMBRIDGE • NEW YORK • SHARJAH

Copyright © Elaine Trimlett Glover (2021)

The right of Elaine Trimlett Glover to be identified as author of this work has been asserted by the author in accordance with section 77 and 78 of the Copyright, Designs and Patents Act 1988.

All rights reserved. No part of this publication may be reproduced, stored in a retrieval system, or transmitted in any form or by any means, electronic, mechanical, photocopying, recording, or otherwise, without the prior permission of the publishers.

Any person who commits any unauthorised act in relation to this publication may be liable to criminal prosecution and civil claims for damages.

All of the events in this memoir are true to the best of author's memory. The views expressed in this memoir are solely those of the author.

A CIP catalogue record for this title is available from the British Library.

ISBN 9781398410800 (Paperback)
ISBN 9781398410817 (ePub e-book)

www.austinmacauley.com

First Published (2021)
Austin Macauley Publishers Ltd
25 Canada Square
Canary Wharf
London
E14 5LQ

I would like to thank Canon Andrew White and his team at Jerusalem Merit, Austin Macauley for believing in my work and all those who have contributed financially; friends, family and sponsors.

Thanks to Mr Raouf and his family who are now my Kurdish family, for their wonderful hospitality and friendship that I will never forget.

Thanks to all my friends, Facebook friends and family who have supported me in the publication of this book financially.

Thanks to Trevor, Pastor Sanjay Sanil, Chris and Christine Welch, Edith, Maureen Julie, Cathy and my husband, Adrian, who have supported me along the way. Not forgetting Sally Gray from USA, who proofread my book.

Thanks to God for answering my prayer and taking me to places I never thought I would go, meet people I never thought I would meet and do things I never thought I would do.

Lastly to Alley Mckay of Middleville, Ontario, Canada, who told me to 'see all, hear all, remember all' and write it down.

Table of Contents

Introduction	12
Chapter 1	16
"Is This All You Have for My Life, Lord"	
Chapter 2	33
Don't Take Care, Take Risks	
Chapter 3	40
Pray! Pray! Pray! Pray!	
Chapter 4	45
The Golden Scarf and the Warrior Bride	
Chapter 5	57
My Trip to Iraq	
Chapter 6	67
Baghdad	
Chapter 7	89
Halabja	

Chapter 8 97

A New Beginning

Chapter 9 105

The Seder Marriage of the Lamb

"Don't Take Care,
Take Risks."

Motto of Canon Andrew White,
'Vicar of Baghdad'

Introduction

When seeking God, one of the most dangerous questions you can ask is, "Is this all you have for my life?" This is exactly what I did, as in 2010 my husband had just passed away, having had muscular dystrophy, and it seemed like my whole world had fallen apart and I felt half of me was missing. I had been Nigel's carer 24/7 and at the same time we also were partners in a ministry for four years, called 'Watering Hole', where we shared the love of Jesus on a deprived estate. Watering Hole was an incentive of 'Redeeming Our Communities' led by Debra Green, where the church, local government, police and community engaged in prayer and action through various projects to lower crime through life transformation in Jesus Christ.

I could have continued with the project, but without Nigel, it was like tea without toast, or salt without pepper. Therefore, now that Nigel had gone to be with the Lord, I had decided to move down south to live near some Christian friends and hopefully have a fresh start.

Many people thought I had run away because of grief whilst others suggested that I was having a midlife crisis, however, God was restoring my foundations and healing me. Being a carer and a director of a project, I was exhausted and so the Lord was restoring me and filling my bucket as I had given so much of myself away to others. God also had a plan for my life, plans to prosper me, not to harm me but to give me a hope and a future.

"For I know the plans I have for you," declares the Lord, *"plans to prosper you and not to harm you, plans to give you hope and a future." (Jeremiah 29: Verse 11).*

First of all, I moved to Hayling Island, Southampton, where I became a relief project worker in the Elderfield, Otterbourne, for Langley House Trust (LHT), which was a project that helped ex-offenders/offenders and people with various needs back into the community. It was in the grounds of the Elderfield that I would pray during my lunch break, as the garden was very beautiful and peaceful.

I remember feeling very low in myself and suicidal as I was still grieving for Nigel and the only answer was to seek the face of God concerning my future as everything seemed to be going pear-shaped. My rented accommodation was up for sale. Every time I applied for a full-time job with LHT, I wasn't successful and my financial situation was getting out of control, especially running a car and having to pay bills as a single person.

"Is this all you have for my life, Lord?" I grumbled to God over and over and over again. "Lord, I have got two jobs and working night and day, and everything is just not working out, Lord, please help me!"

Two weeks later, Canon Andrew White, the famous Vicar of Baghdad, had been led by God to ring me and tell me that I was to host Mr Raouf and his family in the Spires hospital,

Southampton, as he and his wife were both coming to England for an operation. Amazingly, Mr Raouf was the Minister of Justice in Iraq who sentenced Saddam Hussein to death for war crimes in Halabja.

At the same time, I was asked by Heaven on Earth Ministries in Homa Bay, Kenya, to come on mission and so as you can see, my prayer had been clearly answered by God in two weeks. God takes you to places you never thought you would go, meet people you never thought you would meet, and do things you never thought you would do, not in a million years.

This is why God is very unbelievable and miraculous in the way he answers our prayers as you simply couldn't make it up as he does things that are totally out of the box.

"Before I formed thee in the belly I knew thee; and before thou camest forth out of the womb I sanctified thee, and I ordained thee a prophet to the nations." (Jeremiah 1: Verse 5)

God made you and designed you uniquely. He created your character, what you like and don't like. He knows how to meet your desires and what you are good at. He knows everything about us and He also trains us through life experience for the race we run. God is a God who makes ways where there are no ways and his thoughts aren't our thoughts and it's a good thing that they aren't.

God used my street preaching to make me into a preacher and teacher. He used my alcohol addiction as a backslider to lead alcoholics to the Lord. He used my caring skills to host the Iraqi Minister of Justice, and his family. He took my experience as a victim of domestic violence to help ASBO kids, single parents, addicts and those with mental health issues on a deprived estate, and he took my brokenness to give me a heart for the lost.

God had me doing some amazing things, like taking Mr Raouf's daughter and niece to Hillsong Church in the Dominion Theatre, London. He gave me the boldness to travel on my own to Israel, Canada, Iraq, Baghdad and Kenya. God has used me to lead witchdoctors to Christ, minister to the president of Kenya, host funerals and stay with the Judge who sentenced Saddam Hussein, and his family. This is why I have written this book to show you that when you are in God's will, you don't need to be a leader, you don't need to go to Bible school, you don't need to be wealthy or have been to university; all you need is a willing heart, obedience, trust in the Lord and...

"If God tells you to do something, do it!" – Michael Pilavachi.

"Don't take care, take risks." – Canon Andrew White, Vicar of Baghdad.

Chapter 1
"Is This All You Have for My Life, Lord"

Browsing down my Facebook Messenger, I came across a request from Canon Andrew White, the notorious Vicar of Baghdad, to ring him. My first thoughts were, what does he want? I didn't know him and I had only seen him once when he gave a lecture at Leicester University in 2009 where he spoke about his ministry in Baghdad and Iraq. During question time, I asked Andrew if he saw God's healing and experienced answered prayers in his church, St George's, Baghdad? Andrew's reply was quite unforgettable because he spoke about how the Ayatollah (a Shiite leader), desperate to find a way to feed his starving people because of war, asked Andrew for money but Canon Andrew White only had $12 on him at the time. This didn't deter the Iraqi Shiite leader who then asked the Vicar of Baghdad to pray for food because he knew that Andrew's God answered prayers. That night as Andrew finished reading the book of Common Prayer, he suddenly remembered the Ayatollahs request and simply prayed "FOOD!"

The following day as Andrew sat having his breakfast in a hotel, an American high-ranked officer came over asking if he could do anything with 145 tons of meat, in refrigerated articulated lorries, as the US troops had no need for it! God obviously had heard Andrew's prayer for meat and then got to work at not only providing the much-needed food but also he provided a means to keep it fresh and be able to deliver it. The Vicar of Baghdad sat there in amazement at such an offer, then as bells began to ring and the penny dropped, he said, "YES!" He knew exactly what to do with it. This was a miraculous answer to prayer which would not only feed the hungry Iraqi people who were starving but was also an amazing testimony for the Ayatollah.

Andrew also spoke about how eleven Muslim men had become Christians and despite knowing the risk of being murdered by their own families if they discovered about their new faith in Yeshua, they wanted to be baptised. A week later, only two of the eleven men were still alive as the other nine men had been murdered by their Muslim families. According to Muslim belief, Isa (Jesus), was just a prophet and not the Son of God and that Mohammed is THE prophet.

From hearing these incredible testimonies, I knew that Canon Andrew White was a special man of God whose faith was outstanding and had been a huge encouragement to me, this was also why I was so intrigued to find out why he wanted to talk to me and what it was about, and so I rang him.

"Hello, Canon Andrew White, you asked me to phone you. It's Elaine from Facebook."

"Oh yes, Canon Andrew White here. Have you heard of Saddam Hussein?"

"Yes," I replied. I never in a million years expected him to ask if I had heard of Saddam Hussein and wondered if indeed

Andrew was winding me up? "Have you ever seen the judge who sentenced Saddam to death on the television?"

"Yes, I have," I said, wondering what he was going to ask next.

Andrew then began to explain how he himself as a chaplain for the American Embassy in Baghdad had sat in the courtroom during Saddam's trial and the judge, Mr Raouf, had asked the Vicar of Baghdad if he could borrow his green ink pen to sign the official paper and, unknowingly, he let the Minister of Justice borrow his pen, not realising it was going to be used to sign Saddam's death warrant.

A few months after the trial when Saddam had been executed, the Iraqi Minister of Justice, Mr Raouf, rang Andrew to ask him for another favour. Canon Andrew White explained, "Mr Raouf knew that if anybody wanted anything done in Iraq, Abuna (Abuna is the term the children called Canon Andrew which means 'Father' especially in the Middle East Church Community) Andrew could do it." The Judge explained that he needed major surgery on his cervical vertebrae as he had spinal stenosis and his wife had a major break in her foot that wouldn't heal and they wanted me to find a surgeon who could do both operations and at the same time, could speak Aramaic.

As Andrew used to be a 'gas man', an anaesthetist in St Thomas's Hospital, London, in his younger years, he therefore asked some of his contacts if there was a Kurdish surgeon who could not only operate on Mr and Mrs Raouf but who could speak in Aramaic language. He discovered that only three hospitals in the world had a consultant with these requirements and miraculously one of these men, Mr Ali, worked for the Spires Private Hospital in Southampton. I did ask him why he couldn't have the operation in Iraq and Andrew explained, the Iraqi Minister of Justice was very concerned for his life and didn't want his head chopped off.

Canon Andrew White was then left to make all the arrangements for the Judge to come to UK for his hospital treatment as well as Mr Raouf's family's accommodation during their visit. As Andrew was always travelling from Israel to Jordan, and Jordan to Baghdad, he realised he needed someone to help him in Southampton to host the judge and his family. This is why he had prayed to the Lord, "How can I do all of this on my own?"

God replied, "Ask Elaine, she will do it!"

Andrew explained, "I wasn't sure how to approach you as I don't even know you. However, God said to me just ring her up and that's what I am doing."

I couldn't believe what I was hearing and to be honest, you couldn't make it up. I just kept wondering if it was a wind up as it was so out of the box.

Looking back, God had really brought about this miracle after having heard my cry of wanting to do more for His Kingdom and hearing Andrew's cry in his heart for God to send him someone to take the responsibility of hosting Mr Raouf and his Kurdish family, and God simply brought us together.

However, I kept asking God, "Why Me?"

God's reply was, "Why not? It was only the other week when you prayed in the Elderfield, *is this all you have for my life*, moaning about your cleaning job, house up for sale and not being able to get a full-time job. Oh, ye of little faith?"

"Oh yes, Lord, I forgot about that," was my reply. I had no choice but to say to Andrew, "Yes, I will be a host for the Raouf's." Andrew seemed most relieved.

"Was this really happening to me?" I asked myself.

"Why me, Lord? Why me, Lord?" I kept repeating over and over again, totally shocked at what had just transpired.

"Elaine, why not? This is what you have been praying for and now I am giving you more to do in MY Kingdom." God's reply was hardly a joke. He was answering my prayers in ways only he could do.

Before Andrew said good bye, he told me that Gehad, a member of his team, would phone me once the Kurdish family's visas had been approved and all their arrangements had been sorted out. I wasn't really listening to Andrew because when he mentioned the name Jihad, 'struggle, effort,or holy war' came to mind which unnerved me as to what I was letting myself in for. However, when I checked the spelling of Gehad, I saw that it meant 'married man' in English translation and I felt so much more at ease.

Once I put the phone down, I had to tell someone what had just happened and so I rang a friend from my Church who didn't believe me. He, like me, thought it was a joke or I had been scammed on Facebook. When I rang my pastor at the time, Pastor Sanjay Sanil, a godly man from India, he seemed very happy that God was doing something new in my life. I dare not tell my mother though, as I know she wouldn't believe me and she'd warn me not to get involved with these kinds of people, plus she would be very worried and concerned.

God, however, knows me better than I know myself as he created me and is aware that I really do like challenges and adventure and there was no way I would have turned an opportunity like this down because I doubt I would have ever had this 'God job' again.

It also taught me that when you say to God, *Is this all you have for my life,* you are walking on thin ice; as to be honest, you never know where God will send you, what he will do and who you will meet along the way.

"For I know the plans I have for you," declares the Lord, *"plans to prosper you and not to harm you, plans to give you hope and a future." (Jeremiah 29: Verse 11)*

For a long period of time, there seemed great silence, leaving me on tenterhooks with that foreboding feeling that it was all a set-up, as it just seemed so surreal. All I seemed to do was moan and groan as to why Andrew had phoned me up and then left me hanging on a string, wondering what was really going on. However, after a few more weeks of feeling disappointment, Andrew did ring me and told me to call his colleague Gehad to put my mind at rest.

Hardly able to contain myself with excitement, I took a 'Leap of Faith' and rang Gehad who didn't say a great deal but we prayed together about the forthcoming events and he explained a little bit about himself, how he was once a pilot for the Iraqi Air Force during the Iraq war. Gehad also explained that it was during the war years that he had met Canon Andrew White, and then became an Arabic and English translator after the war. Andrew gave him a job in his Foundation for Relief and Reconciliation in the Middle East (FRRME).

It reassured me greatly, knowing that this adventure was real, with real people. Then after a few more weeks of silence, I took another brave 'Leap of Faith' and rang Gehad again. This time he seemed more open and we ended up talking, laughing and joking about all sorts of things, for ages. However, the next few weeks, one minute it was GREEN for GO! And then it was RED and sadly not on at all. I did wonder if it was down to security reasons or Mr Raouf and his family couldn't get visas to come to the UK, which I now realise isn't easy. However, it was very frustrating as I needed to book some time off of work to be able to host the Kurdish family as well as juggle shifts to suit and I was getting a bit stressed. After praying, all I could hear was God saying, "O my child, oh ye of little faith!"

Eventually, after a very long waiting game and round of phone calls as to when and where we would meet, I found myself armed with chocolates and presents to give to Andrew and his friends, plus flowers for the judge's wife. As it was the first time I had met any of these people properly, I took my good friend Trevor with me from West End Church for accountability.

Both Trevor and I were rather nervous, wondering what was going to happen at the Hilton Hotel, in Southampton, when we all met, as it still seemed to be too far-fetched to be real. However, God is in the business of 'far-fetched' and 'out of the box' if you simply trust in him.

As we walked in the Hilton Hotel reception, I had to pinch myself as my eyes glanced towards the sofa and saw the famous Canon Andrew White, the Vicar of Baghdad, the man I heard giving a lecture in Leicester University. Andrew was a very tall well-dressed and well-built man who carried the presence of God.

Besides him was a man who looked like the 1980s American TV Police Detective 'Kojak' with a bald head, who turned out to be Mr Raouf, the judge who sentenced Saddam Hussein to death.

Standing on the opposite side of the Vicar of Baghdad, was a very tall stocky man with glasses, called Ken and although he had a good sense of humour, you knew you wouldn't and couldn't mess with him. I thought Ken was Andrew's bodyguard from MI5 at first but actually Ken was Andrew's driver and right-hand man.

Standing up behind Mr Raouf was another man, quite small and stocky, who wore a light brown mac and looked like 1980s TV Detective 'Columbo', who was none other than Gehad. He certainly was not the shy person who I had spoken to several times on the phone but he indeed had a big personality with a great sense of humour, which was why he and Ken seemed to bounce off each other with their jokes and witty comments. Andrew's group also consisted of a very well-dressed, well-spoken and polite young man, who was a PA of Andrew. Whilst in Mr Raouf's group were his two beautiful daughters, both well-dressed, very slim and gracious, especially the eldest daughter. Mrs Raouf was meant to have joined us but was sleeping in their hotel room because she was so tired and her ankle caused her a lot of pain, especially after such a long journey.

All I could do was pinch myself as I couldn't believe this was happening but more than that, I was in awe of the people I had just been introduced to, especially Mr Raouf and Canon Andrew White who are both in the limelight as powerful men in their own right. Mr Raouf's eldest daughter really impressed me as she gave Andrew a beautiful rug of the 'Last Supper' as a gift. In my eyes, it was a remarkable, wonderful recognition and acknowledgement of the Christian faith by a Sunni Muslim. This is what the Vicar of Baghdad deals with, reconciliation and working for peace, why this beautiful lady was so thoughtful and wise. Really all I could do was pinch myself, thinking, *Wow, am I really here?*

When the waiter came to take orders for drinks, hot chocolate was the order of the day. It was Mr Raouf's family's favourite drink, a Middle East speciality and so I ordered a hot chocolate too and used this time to give out presents to the family, such as chocolates and flowers. With only Mrs Raouf's flowers left to hand out, I asked her eldest daughter to give them to her mum once she had rested in the room. She explained that her mother had had a car accident and was hoping that this fifth operation on her broken ankle would be a success as the pain was getting too much to cope with.

Both groups thanked me for the gifts but despite being a generous person, it had been the Holy Spirit who had directed me to bring presents and now I understand why, as hospitality and generosity is a part of their Kurdish culture. God was at work building relationships!

Mr Raouf,
Iraqi Minster of Justice, and
Canon Andrew White,
the Vicar of Baghdad.

This is when I began to see why God had chosen me to host the family as I realised God wanted me to pray for the Kurdish family for their salvation, healing and successful operations, whilst building up good relationships with them. This task needed great wisdom as they were not only Kurdish but also Sunni Muslims from Halabja and Mr Raouf was the Iraqi Minister of Justice involved with politics in Iraq and his daughters were his secretaries. I just couldn't believe that God had chosen me as I felt so unworthy but looking back, he had been training me for such a time as this over the past several years of obedience and my love for prayer whilst being bold for God, just like Canon Andrew White's motto, "Don't take care, but take risks!"

It was indeed a historical moment in time that you couldn't make up and one of which few people would believe or understand. From a security point of view, although security must have taken place, the Kurdish family's stay in Southampton would be relatively safe compared to having something like this in Baghdad, as then it would have been a whole different ball game.

One of the reasons why I wanted to look after the Kurdish family was because before Nigel died, we were in a situation that saw us stuck in a hotel, after our van broke down on the M3 at the Winchester service station as the fuel pump was broken. Thanks to Frank Brooks late, founding member of 'Transformed Ministries', people like Grace, a Christian from Southampton, began to pray for us and arranged for different people to come and visit us in our hotel. A wonderful couple who were on the Transformed Trustees board, not only visited us but also paid for our hotel bill. Therefore, it only seemed right for me to assist the Vicar of Baghdad by hosting the Kurdish family whilst they were in hospital. When you are in a place where you don't know anybody, it can be very lonely, isolating and cause depression and great fear. This is why for me, yes it was a great honour to serve God in this way.

From now on, it was my task to make them feel at home, cared for and loved, plus my prayer was for God to make ways for me to pray for Mr and Mrs Raouf and for them to have successful operations. I needed the full armour of God and humility, grace, faith, mercy, obedience, kindness and wisdom, as it was a massive responsibility. Before I continued with the task God had given me, I wanted to find out a little more about Andrew and Mr Raouf so that I wasn't going into this blind, but prepared and spiritually anointed.

However, the more I found out about these two men, the more I felt unworthy and frightened at the task ahead and the responsibility, plus all the questions of would I be followed by terrorist and get shot? Would Mr Raouf and his family want me to pray for them and how would they react to my testimonies and love for Jesus as they were Muslims?

But God didn't give me a spirit of fear but of love, faith and hope, which is why I stopped asking so many questions and thinking so much, trying to analyse everything, and got on with the job that God had given me and trust in Him. All I could do was my best, with God at the helm.

I held on to Canon Andrew White's motto, "Don't take care, take risks", and the scripture in the Bible, Mark 4: verse 37–41, where there was a storm brewing up and as Jesus slept, the disciples were afraid and complaining their master was asleep. They woke him up and Jesus commanded the storm to be calm and rebuked the disciples by saying, *"Where is your faith?"*

Raouf Abdul Rahman,
Minister of Justice, Chief Judge, who sentenced Saddam
Hussein to death for chemical war crimes in Halabja 1988.

I discovered that the man whom I would be hosting was the replacement for Mr Rizgar as Chief Judge of the Supreme Iraqi Criminal Tribunal of Saddam Hussein, on 23rd January 2006. Mr Rizgar was apparently seen as too soft and could easily give Saddam Hussein and his men a much too lenient sentence for the war crimes he had committed. Mr Raouf, however, wouldn't suffer fools gladly, as he was an ethnic Kurd from Halabja, born in 1941. Both he and his family were subjected to Saddam's gas attack on this city in 1988 and who, by the grace of God, escaped to Iran until it was safe to return to Iraq. Looking back, God used Chief Judge Raouf 'as a means to bring about justice for the mass genocide of his community, the Kurdish people in Halabja, as Mr Raouf not only sentenced Saddam Hussein to death but also some of Saddam's top aides.

During the trial, Saddam Hussein, a very intimidating and evil despot, known for his evil and merciless exploits, shouted out loudly in court, "I AM the president of Iraq," and, "WHAT CAN YOU DO TO ME?"

Iraq's Minster of Justice, Chief Judge, Mr Raouf, only five foot-something tall, calmly stated, "I AM president of this court so kindly SIT DOWN AND SHUT UP!"

This empowered the Kurdish people, which gave Mr Raouf their total respect and rightly so!

Canon Andrew White
Vicar of Baghdad

As I did some research on Andrew, I was totally astounded by what I read on 'Google'. Andrew grew up in Bexley, Kent, and his family were very unique, as his parents were strict Pentecostal and strict Baptist. Andrew himself was very unique, as when asked what he wanted to be when he grew up, he replied he wanted to be a doctor and a vicar, of which the teacher said he could only be one.

However, as he grew up, he proved his teacher wrong because he became an Anaesthetist 'a gas man', with the cardiac arrest team whilst studying at Thomas's Hospital in London. Then once he had achieved what he had set out to do, he asked God what next and God told him to become an Anglican Vicar just as he had predicted.

Andrew studied theology and trained for the priesthood at Ridley Hall, Cambridge, where he studied the Abrahamic faiths, studying at the Hebrew University, Jerusalem. In 1990, he was ordained as a Curate at St Mark's in Battersea, Southwark, London. During this time, he was interviewed by Esther Rantzen whilst dancing with an umbrella in the pouring rain, singing, "I'm singing in the rain."

This was to be his first claim to fame as the televised sketch was used on 'That's Life's' opening clip, which is why he became known as the 'Singing Vicar' who was an ardent fan of 'That's Life'; I can remember it well. All those years later, who would have thought he would ring me up for a special assignment from God?

Southwark must have been a special place for Andrew as it was here in his congregation that he met his wife, Caroline. I remember him telling me that as he preached from the pulpit, his eyes met Caroline's and he fell madly in love with her. Six weeks later, Andrew asked her to marry him and she initially said, "Maybe," but of course, she eventually said, "Yes," and they later married and had two children, Josiah and Jacob.

After becoming the Vicar of the Church of the Ascension, Balham Hill, in the same diocese, in 1997, his final year as Vicar there, he became a Councillor of Wandsworth Borough Council and served as deputy Chairman of Social Services.

1998, Andrew was appointed a Canon at Coventry Cathedral, not long after his brother had committed suicide in 1997. Six weeks later, the same day as Jacob was born, Andrew received some more tragic news that he had been diagnosed with MS.

However, that wasn't going to deter him with God's plan, as he became the director of an international ministry there, heading up the International Centre for Reconciliation. It was here that Andrew promoted reconciliation in conflicts (mainly religious) across the globe, concentrating on the Middle East because he thought that the church needed to be involved there and empowered.

He remained in this post until 2005, when he moved to Baghdad to become Anglican Chaplain to Iraq where he was commonly known as 'the Vicar of Baghdad' or 'Abuna' to the locals who attended St George's Church, the only Anglican Church in Baghdad. The Foundation for Relief and Reconciliation in the Middle East was established in 2005 as part of his reconciliation work in Iraq and the Middle East as a whole.

His main aim has been to try to maintain communication between Shiite and Sunni leaders and to "gain the trust of key religious leaders on both sides in various conflict areas". He saw his role as trying to mediate and re-establish the dialogue between conflicting groups.

He also took part in trying to resolve the hostage situation at the Church of the Nativity in Bethlehem in 2002. I remember Andrew telling me how he and his co-worker Hanna were involved in a head-on collision with an Israeli tank and the first thing Hanna asked the soldiers was, "Do you have insurance?"

The more I read, the more I realised the kind of people I would be working with and the more humbling it became and the more exciting as the sense of danger and adventure was becoming more apparent. I still kept having to pinch myself after hearing that Andrew's lay pastor had been kidnapped and he was involved with the hostage negotiations raising $40,000 for the 'Lay Pastor's' release. I also read that Canon Andrew White had been kidnapped and released himself after being held in a room full of chopped-off fingers.

Canon Andrew White, wasn't only seen as being a 'hero' but he had been appointed as a replacement Envoy from to the Middle East, winning the Anglo-Israel Association Prize for his contribution to furthering understanding between the British and Israeli nations. Andrew was also a well-known author of many books including. 'My Story so Far, Faith Under Fire.'

"Goodness me, Elaine, what has God got in store for you?" I asked myself, but I was truly up for all God had for me in His wonderful Kingdom.

Chapter 2
Don't Take Care, Take Risks

Andrew was speaking at Cosham Baptist Church, one Sunday to promote his work and raise funds for his work in Baghdad. At the same time, he wanted me to come along to the service to meet a man called 'Brian the Squirrel', who was also helping Andrew with Mr Raouf's visit. Andrew knew Brian, from Brian's ministry with the Kurdish community in Portsmouth. He was also responsible for placing a plaque in Southsea Park, to commemorate those who died in Saddam's chemical attack in Halabja, where Mr Raouf came from.

Sunday evening, I arrived at the church really early so as to give me a chance to have a coffee and biscuits whilst talking and praying for some people from the church who were going out on mission. Afterwards, I went and sat in the chapel to listen to the worship music which was wonderful and as Andrew and Ken arrived chatting to members of the church and selling some of his books, I came across Brian the Squirrel. I expected him to be tall, and suited and booted, yet he was a small man with glasses, wearing shorts. I later discovered that Brian's shorts were his trademark which he was famous for. However, Brian was also well-known for having a real massive heart for the Kurdish people and also for God.

Brian told me that the first time he had flown to Baghdad, he was turned back for having no visa and so he rang Andrew at St George's for help. Andrew asked him how he got to Baghdad Airport and if he had a visa. Brian simply explained that Jesus had sent him. Brian had to fly to Erbil where he was greeted by a phone call from Andrew who arranged some of his people to pick Brian up and drive him back to St George's, which must have been a very brave and courageous thing to do but he didn't take care, he took risks. His God was with him. Since then, he had met with the judge and family and has been to Baghdad several times which is why as Mr Raouf and his family had originated from Halabja, Brian wanted to show the judge the memorial plaque in his people's honour, most likely why God chose Brian as he did me…

After taking the service, giving a sermon about Joseph and his dreams, Andrew and Brian asked me where we could take the judge for a Kurdish meal. I didn't really know Southampton that well so I looked in the phone book and came across one in Saint Mary's. However, I was told it wasn't a very nice area to take the Minister of Justice and so I had a look on 'Google' again and came up with a Thai restaurant in Southampton Docks. In the end, Brian made the suggestion that we take Mr Raouf, and his nephew to lunch to a family-run Kurdish restaurant, which was not far away from the park in Southsea. We decided that's what we would do, as it was far more practical for many reasons.

Brian's Jesus Van.
On convoy to a Portsmouth Kurdish Restaurant,
with myself, Brian, Gehad,
Mr Raouf and Canon Andrew White and Ken.
(The two men most wanted by ISIS.
With over $90 million worth on their heads.)

The following day, I drove to the hospital in my vintage Green Volvo, which was an embarrassment, plus I wasn't very good at parking at the best of times. What made the situation even worse, was that I struggled to find a parking space and ended up having no choice but to park up the curb, otherwise I wouldn't have been able to visit Mr Raouf at all. On arrival, I could see my new friends looking out the window of the hospital reception which made me very nervous, and I was hoping that they hadn't seen my parking skills in such a big car. However, I sat opposite Andrew, Mr Raouf and 'Brian the Squirrel' as we waited for the pre-operation appointment. Sat next to Mr Raouf was his nephew who had joined his famous uncle to escort him not only to his appointment but to visit the Halabja Memorial Plaque in Southsea.

Ken and Gehad started laughing and joking as we chatted amongst ourselves and the atmosphere was really happy, as the joy of the Lord was indeed our strength. The humorous outburst was very catching and it broke the ice and stopped the worry of meeting the consultant and what Mr Ali was going to tell them. Before we set off, Ken had to help me remove a very large boulder which had lodged itself underneath my vehicle and I couldn't move backwards or forwards. I was totally stuck but praise God, Ken really did wonders and lifted the car off the curb and over the boulder. Another bit of excitement, I expect, for the visitors at Spires Hospital Southampton. If the event had been captured on video, it would have made good TV. In fact, the whole convoy to Portsmouth to have lunch at a Kurdish Restaurant was so funny, you would think it was a comedy show.

In front of the convoy was Ken in his blacked-out four-by-four, driving Mr Raouf's nephew, Canon Andrew White and Mr Raouf—ISIS' two most wanted men with at least $90,000,000,00 price tag on their heads between them.

Brian was driving behind them in his Squirrel's Jesus flag waving at its bonnet. Whilst behind Brian was me in my big clapped-out Green Volvo with the worship song, 'Our God is greater, our God is stronger higher than any other,'" blaring away out of my window but whether anyone could hear it, I don't know. Behind me was Gehad in a small blue car. I just wondered what a passer-by must have thought and I always wondered if they actually had any security.

Before we arrived at the restaurant, we passed Brian's antique shop and on the window was a board with 'JESUS' written over it. What a witness and God knew what he was doing when he told Andrew that Brian and myself were to look after the Kurdish family but I did wonder what Mr Raouf's thoughts were at being a prominent Sunni Muslim figure in Iraq? You honestly couldn't make it up but that was the beauty of God's mastermind plan so no one would guess what was going on or believe it for that matter.

As usual, parking was a bit of an issue for me and this time it was Gehad's turn to come to the rescue and park my Volvo into a very tight space. Once everyone had parked, we all trundled into the Kurdish restaurant that Brian had booked. Once the waiters had pushed two tables together to accommodate our group, we sat down and had some wonderful Kurdish food. As the Kurdish family was Muslim, Brian chose this restaurant as they offered lots of well-known Halal Kurdish dishes, such as falafel, humus and kebabs. To start off with, we had a yogurt drink, made out of yogurt, salt, water and mint. This was a very acquired taste as the first sip was very salty, most likely why Andrew put sugar in his and plenty of it. However, I remember I had had this drink before in Turkey where it was used for an antidote for hangovers or to recover from food poisoning as the ingredients replaced the body fluids lost in being sick.

Brian prayed the grace before we started demolishing the starter, which consisted of lots of dips, salad and flat bread similar to Indian Nan bread. Then the main course consisted of more salad, lots of halal chicken and lamb but we didn't have any pork for obvious reasons, followed by the dessert, which was segments of orange and Turkish coffee or hot chocolate, to finish the meal off. Gehad and Ken continued their banter, both having an excellent sense of humour which gave me a real feeling of belonging, something I hadn't felt since Nigel died. To be honest after having such a lovely humorous time with genuine friendly people, eating lovely food, I didn't want the day to end. Sadly, I had to leave to start a shift at Langley House Trust. Mr Raouf and his nephew were very keen to visit the Halabja Memorial Plaque, which Brian and his Kurdish Association had placed at the Southsea Park to commemorate all those who died in Halabja.

Mr Raouf at the 'Halabja Memorial Plaque' Southsea, Portsmouth. Commemorating all those who died in Saddam's chemical attack Halabja.

Chapter 3
Pray! Pray! Pray! Pray!

The day of Mr Raouf's operation, I had told Gehad that I wanted to pray for Mr Raouf before he had his operation. We both waited in the reception area until we were able to pray with him for a successful operation. It was a very risky operation that Mr Raouf was about to have on his spine. It was also going to be a very difficult job for his consultant to perform such an operation on his neck as the Consultant Mr Ali, had to go through the front of the neck to get to the vertebrae. If it went wrong, it could cause terrible problems for the Minister of Justice, even paralysis, and yet it was his wish to leave the hospital as soon as he could to go back to work. I must admit, it was very miraculous and a privilege to be praying for such an important man from Middle East history; as in reality, a Sunni Muslim man wouldn't let a woman pray for him, never mind a Christian.

Mr Raouf's two daughters really enjoyed all the humour among us, especially in the hospital reception, as the joy of the Lord remained our strength. It must have been a worry for Mr Raouf and his family as to what the outcome of his surgery would be. However, I firmly believe that Mr Raouf had a faith in Andrew's God, just like the Ayatollah did through the testimony of Andrew's life and answered prayer.

Knowing that it was a difficult time, I had bought some more presents for the family, some purses for the daughters, pens and get-well cards with scripture written inside them for Mr and Mrs Raouf. I wasn't trying to score brownie points, but simply all I wanted to do was to share the love of God to this family who were away from their family and friends in another country, whilst having complicated major surgery.

As I waited for Mr Raouf to be taken to surgery, I met Mrs Raouf for the first time, who clearly was very concerned about her husband. I could see concern in her face, which is why I felt great compassion for Mrs Raouf as I knew what it was like to wait for someone to come back from major surgery.

My late husband Nigel had a 'pacemaker' fitted in his heart and I spent the whole afternoon in the Chapel, praying to Yeshua, whilst singing Godfrey Birtill worship songs. You worry when they are taken into theatre and then you cry with relief when they are wheeled back to the ward alive and in one piece. Mrs Raouf and myself couldn't speak each other's languages but we clearly did understand each other very well.

Mr Raouf, after a long time, was wheeled upstairs by a porter to get ready for his operation, with his wife, two daughters and nephew by his side, showing their support. In the meantime, Gehad and I remained downstairs for a few hours, chatting away and laughing, yet underneath we were both concerned if Mr Raouf would pull through the risky operation. After a long time of waiting about, Gehad went upstairs to check on how Mr Raouf was and if he had gone to theatre, with me in hot pursuit. Looking at the clock, I asked Gehad if he would translate for me and ask Mr and Mrs Raouf if it was alright for me to pray for them. I was worried in case they were offended, although I knew God had told me to have faith. When Gehad did ask the Kurdish couple if I could pray with them, they both agreed.

I began to ask God for His healing, restoration and peace over their lives and that the outcome of surgery would be very positive and successful.

Mrs Raouf was quite emotional when I prayed for them and I felt that a shift in the spiritual atmosphere had taken place. Before her husband was wheeled to surgery, Mrs Raouf spent time in prayer alone for her husband, using her subha prayer beads which are similar to a crucifix. However, Sapper beads had more beads than the crucifix. Mr Raouf and his wife were both very spiritual people, which is why I wondered if they were Sufi Muslims because of their love and their spirituality.

Normally, the NHS generally only allows two people in a room at one time to sit in chairs by the patient's bedside, why the atmosphere is normally quite dismal and boring. However, in the Spires private ward, I was amazed to see that Mr Raouf was allowed several visitors in his room at any one time. They were even allowed to eat their own food. Mrs Raouf told me to sit down and passed me some salad with falafel that she had brought with her in a bag. She also offered me fresh herbs which weren't just one or two small leaves but huge clumps of leaves and their stems. I thought to myself, *Does she really want me to eat them like that?* Thankfully, they were surprisingly very tasty in flat bread, washed down with their favourite hot chocolate drink which they had prepared.

You would never have imagined in a million years we would all be having such a lovely, happy and humorous time waiting for Mr Raouf to come back from surgery. I must say it did seem bizarre but apparently in Kurdistan, the whole street came out in support when someone goes to hospital, or when there is a family crisis. In the UK where the family is nucleus, nobody seems to care about each other in the same way, especially when it comes to their aged parents. In my experience, the only time neighbours come out to see what's going on is to moan about where you parked your car, or placed your dustbin.

When Mr Raouf came out of surgery, the most amazing thing happened, as yet again, God had opened a way for me to pray for him with the help of Gehad's translation skills. God really is so amazing and the God of the 'Impossible'. From this point on, Mr Raouf was no longer the Judge who sentenced Saddam, but he had become my dear friend, as was his wife and family, who I thought most highly of and who I was honoured to be able to pray for and look after.

I couldn't visit the Raouf family every day at Spires Hospital as I had my contracted hours to work at Langley House Trust. However, I did explain to my boss, Anne, what was happening and she was quite sympathetic, although I wasn't sure if they believed me or not. Normally, I did as many hours as I could for the Trust, for me to be able to pay the bills but at this point of time, I was needed at the hospital for sake of the Kingdom of God. The more I visited the Raouf family, the more time I wanted to spend with them to pray for healing, salvation and restoration.

During that week, I received a pleasant phone call from Andrew, explaining how Mr Raouf had experienced God in the operating theatre, especially as his operation went so well. The Raouf family certainly believed, it was indeed a great success and we all believed God was certainly very present in that side ward. The joy of the Lord really came down upon us, with power and God was answering our prayers of healing. If God hadn't been with us, then who knows what could have happened, but God was with us and He performed miracle after miracle…

Chapter 4

The Golden Scarf and the Warrior Bride

During this time, I was in a tight financial position. I could pay for food and personal items but didn't have enough money to pay my rent and I knew that God wanted me to sell my jewellery, including my wedding ring and Nigel's thick gold bracelet, as a means to survive. It was a combination of obedience and sacrifice, knowing that this was something I had to do to continue to live and do what God had told me to do, which was looking after the Raouf family.

However, God really showed His love for me because when I was about to leave the hospital, Mrs Raouf gave me one of her own personal rings, and it was like God had acknowledged my obedience with the work He that he had ordained me to do. I was so very blessed by God's love and mercy. Mrs Raouf also gave me her beautiful scarf with gold threads and I began to realise that God had done this so I could take the beautiful scarf to the Warrior Bride Conference, near where I lived in West End, Southampton. Once people had prayed over it, like Paul prayed over a handkerchief, I could take it to the Spires Hospital and place it over Mrs Raouf's ankle before the operation.

When I first went to West End, Southampton, God had instructed me to preach at least once a week at the corner of the little row of shops by the main road. Unbeknown to me, it was opposite where the conference was going to be held. I was also declaring God's Lordship over West End and over a house on the corner of the main road, where there were brick goblins and strange demonic faces on the chimney pots at each end of the house.

Looking back, this was God making preparation in the spiritual realm for this charismatic and prophetic conference 'Warrior Bride'. I didn't know at the time that West End village had a witches' coven and was notorious for its witchcraft practices. Once when I had come home from preaching in the village, I opened the cupboard door and to my horror, the door slammed in my face on its own, so I knew Satan wasn't very happy with me and now I know why!

The day before the conference, at the back of the Community Centre, I saw that some conifer cones had been placed around the beacon which I thought could have been witchcraft activity. Rather than get angry, I got my box of 'Promises of God' scripture and placed one into every cone and then took the cones and made them into the shape of a cross. In the meantime, I prayed that if anyone who touched the cones would be blessed by God and receive salvation. At the same time, the Community Centre, was home to a local church which sadly saw a church split in leadership the weekend before, and so to prevent any spiritual darkness, I prayed for forgiveness, lifting a dark cloud over the place.

'Warrior Bride' was a prophetic conference where we, as the 'Body of Christ,' would be praying for our cities and our Nation and the 'Nations of the World'; therefore, it seemed only natural to pray for Mr and Mrs Raouf and also for the Kurdish Iraqi and Baghdad people and their communities. Mrs Thampy, a well-known prophetic evangelist with her own TV show, was coming from India to speak at this event, as were many other prayer warriors from all over the place.

It would indeed be a powerhouse for the Lord, which is why so many people attended, as they longed for the Glory of the Lord to come down, which it did. I was praying in the Spirit and singing in tongues when the Lord said to me to place the Iraq Minister of Justice's wife's scarf on the Israel flag and then place the Cross on the top of both of them. I just wondered and laughed to myself as if Mr Raouf had seen me prostrate on the floor over an Israeli flag, a cross and the scarf his wife had given me, he would have been horrified. Later on, at the 'Warrior Bride' Conference, a lady told me that what I was doing was interceding on behalf of the Kurdish family to receive salvation, as well as interceding on behalf of the Iraqi people and their land.

God also asked me to get everyone at the conference to pray for Mr Raouf and his wife for their healing and salvation and to pray for Iraq and the Middle East. If Mr Raouf repented and gave his life and heart to Jesus, could you imagine what a powerful testimony he would have and the massive impact it would have on the people of Iraq and Kurdistan?

Whilst I was at the conference, I bumped into the lovely couple who had paid for Nigel and my hotel bill, having been stranded in Southampton after our car had broken down in the main M3 Winchester service station just before Nigel had died. They seemed so fed up and low in spirit because they felt redundant in God's Kingdom and so I had to share with them how their act of kindness had inspired me to help the

Iraqi Minister of Justice and his wife whilst they were in Southampton, needing support whilst having operations. This testimony helped them see a more realistic picture of what they had been doing for the Kingdom of God. At the same time, a young man at the conference also shared with the couple how their financial seed had enabled him to go to Lee Abbey with Bob Light's congregation. This is where he'd given his heart to Jesus and received life-changing salvation. His testimony didn't just bless and restore their confidence in their serving, but it blessed the whole congregation.

The highlight of the conference for me was to see several children giving their testimony of how they met with Jesus in the park. To show these young boys that He was who He said He was, Jesus sent a dove to one boy who, with another boy, found a real sword in a bush, both supernatural events. At the end of the conference, all the children took turns to blow my shofar that I had brought along with me and we all believed and praised God for 'The Revival' He would bring to West End.

The next day, I went to Portsdown Community Church in Havant, where I used to go to whilst I lived in Hayling Island. I managed to get Pastor Peter Stott, to pray for the Kurdish couple, after wrapping the scarf around the cross with the 'Israeli flag', 'Redeemer flag' and 'I am flag'. It was so powerful, yet I could never explain for one minute why all this was happening. I wanted the whole church to hear what God had been doing in my life and pray as a whole congregation for Mr and Mrs Raouf. I must say meeting these prominent and important people didn't happen every day. I could have shouted this from the rooftops but people just didn't get it, they really didn't get it, and most of all, they didn't believe me. Every time I tried to share this entire experience in the church, nobody wanted to know. They didn't see what was happening or taking place in the spirit realm, they didn't understand its importance and possibilities why I left the church feeling very, very frustrated as God had laid them on my heart so strongly. Maybe God was using this as a means of protection to keep the Raouf family safe? It was almost like God had put up a barrier to shield them from sight. I so longed for Mr Raouf and his wife to become Christians and seeing them healed. I put every hour I had and every effort into taking care of them. So much so, I was carrying an enormous burden for both them and Baghdad.

I had to totally rely on the Holy Spirit for guidance as I didn't quite understand the enormity of all of this or what was going on. I just had to put my trust in God and stop questioning. Sadly, as much as the scarf had been given to me by Mrs Raouf, I realised I had to give the scarf back to her, which could be very tricky if handled wrongly as she could be very offended. However, the scarf was like Paul's anointed handkerchief, it carried an anointing to pass on healing from those who had prayed for her, and so I asked Gehad to help me with translation so there would be less likelihood of offence. I wanted to give Mr Raouf's wife a clear understanding as to how I had taken the scarf to the 'Warrior Bride' Conference as a way to carry powerful prayer from those who attended the conference to be passed on to her so she could receive healing, which is why I was giving it back to my Kurdish friend before the operation. I even managed to get a copy of a 'Warrior Bride' Conference pamphlet with photos of those who had prayed for her to make it real and plausible.

Before telling Mrs Raouf about the scarf, we went to Southampton Docks to the Thai Restaurant, to mark the miraculous success of Mr Raouf's operation. I drove Gehad and the judge's nephew to the beautiful restaurant. Ken took Mr and Mrs Raouf, their two daughters and a niece plus Andrew in his big black four-by-four. The Thai food was great. We had all sorts of things, dips and fried vegetables, chicken, lamb and rice. The view of the coastline did help the ambiance, as did our usual two comedians. The great humour and laughter showed us that the joy of the Lord had fallen upon us, as it had throughout their whole trip.

After the meal, Gehad explained to Mrs Raouf why I wanted to return the scarf to her after having so many people pray over it. Mrs Raouf, being very spiritual herself, seemed to be very blessed and encouraged by what Gehad had told her, understanding that I did this as an act of faith for her healing.

This is why I believe that when she finally did have the operation, she placed the scarf over her legs before being taken down to the operating theatre and during her recuperation.

Over those few weeks whilst the couple were in hospital, every time we were gathered together in the private hospital room, the joy of the Lord fell upon us over and over again. We were laughing and joking, discussing all sorts of things. I told them I was a Street Pastor at Hedge End. and described what the role of a Street Pastor was. However, they couldn't understand why Street Pastors would hand out flip flops to girls to prevent them from treading on glass after they had taken their high-heeled shoes off when coming out of a night club.

In their country and in any Muslim country, girls found to be going to a night club and coming out in a drunken state, wearing high-heeled shoes and next to nothing, would be whipped or stoned according to 'Sharia law.' Mr Raouf believed we were encouraging the girls to drink alcohol and was horrified; and to be honest, he was right in his train of thought. I had to explain we were trying to offer help and deter them from being drunk and when I asked Mr Raouf his thoughts, he stated that when an act of kindness comes from the heart, it can't be a bad thing. But to be honest, I knew he wasn't impressed or happy about girls going out drinking and getting drunk.

I also discussed with him about how some men and women in prison had come to faith and their life had been changed 180° through repentance, salvation and transformation in Jesus Christ. Despite Mr Raouf being a Sunni Muslim, he understood about salvation and life transformation, especially being the Minister of Justice because he replied that even a bad Muslim needs to change his behaviour by 180°.

When Mrs Raouf had to go into the operating theatre, and you could tell the love between the Kurdish couple, because when Mr Raouf was having his operation, his wife would go to a quiet place and pray with her Sapper beads and when Mr Raouf's wife was having her operation, he would sit quietly, worrying how she was and he prayed for her using his Sapper beads.

Once Mr Raouf knew that his wife was alright and had come out of the operating theatre in one piece and she was fine, he went back to Iraq, wearing a special support collar around his neck to keep it secure as he had very important work to do as the Minister of Justice in Iraq. However, he made me promise to look after his wife and make sure she returned to him in one piece and this was a job I couldn't say no to as I loved them both with all my heart. To see the Iraqi Minister of Justice going back to work in only two months after such dangerous surgery was truly miraculous. Truly the hand of God was on his life and I knew that Mr Raouf knew that too.

Through these conversations I had with Mr Raouf, I found him to be one of the wisest and most interesting men I have come across because he knew what he believed. He was firm but very fair; although I knew you would never mess with a man like him. Both Mr Raouf and Canon Andrew White were the most amazing men I have ever come across and I thank God for the opportunity to have met them both.

Mrs Raouf, her eldest daughter and myself had a really precious time over the next few days, talking, laughing, eating and praying in the hospital's private room, where they even had a television to keep them amused. One day whilst I was taking a short work break in the ground of Elderfield, the Lord told me to take some flowers and a bowl of fresh blackcurrants, gooseberries and raspberries to Mrs Raouf which they enjoyed. It was so nice to see the two ladies happy and to see a wonderful relationship of friendship developing that went beyond faith and two different cultures to that of respect and kindness.

Once Mrs Raouf left the hospital, I did visit her in London whilst she was staying with her sister and two children. I had an amazing time with the Ralph family again as the joy of the Lord continued to be our strength. Mrs Raouf's sister made me some lovely Kurdish food, whilst her daughter and two nieces took me out to London for the day. They were so kind and bought me some clothes, including a beautiful dress at a Wallis sale so that I could wear it when I went to Kenya. It was like an animal print, all yellow and black and red and green, it was beautiful…

One Sunday, I even had the privilege to take Mr Raouf's daughter and niece with me to Hillsong United Church in the Dominion Theatre, London. What was so encouraging was that Mrs Raouf's daughter enjoyed the preaching because she had read about the Bible character he was talking about in the Koran. They also enjoyed the music. I couldn't believe what I was witnessing and seeing such amazing miracles. It showed me the power of God in a way that I had never seen before. Whilst I was visiting the family, I even got to meet the Ambassador for Iraq, Mr Lukman, and being an Iraqi Christian, he allowed me to pray with him. Why the Lord to me was truly amazing!

A few weeks later when Mrs Raouf's cast was taken off and it was clear to everyone that her foot looked so much better than it had been, especially once the bruising had gone, she was told that she wouldn't be in pain as she was before. This was clearly the hand of God and I was so pleased I had been obedient to the Holy Spirit and taken the golden scarf to the Warrior Bride Conference and Portsdown Community Church as God had answered our prayers.

Elaine in Elderfield garden where she prayed and made a beautiful bouquet of flowers for Mrs Raouf.

I also went to visit Andrew, fondly known as 'Abuna' (priest or father), at his home in Liphook on his birthday and discovered his office is truly magnificent as he has over 400 crosses hanging up on every wall in his office. They range from a cross that was made just after Jesus' crucifixion to a present-day cross. The crosses came from all over the world and from all sorts of people, especially from the Middle East, and some were big crosses, some small, in all sorts of shapes and designs. Andrew showed me his Muslim wall with pictures, crosses and photos, then a Jewish wall, and finally a

Christian wall with photos of Andrew with various Presidents and Prime Ministers, which were altogether a living history.

Andrew had lots of books and pictures in his office, even one of Muslims praying in Cairo and one of Saddam Hussein with a soldier standing next to him. I know God has a sense of humour when Andrew explained that after Saddam was arrested, his chair was given to the Chaplain of Baghdad, which he was. However, although he sat on it, Andrew made it known that he is a very busy man and doesn't have time to sit down...

For his birthday, I had bought him the 'Lord's Prayer' Cross from Jerusalem which I had just purchased from the Garden tomb whilst on holiday. Moreover, knowing he liked cakes, I bought him four birthday cakes from the local bakery in West End—a lemon cake, coffee cake, a walnut cake and a chocolate cake—to make sure I bought him one he liked. He went for the lemon cake, which he said was delicious. We also had a cup of tea from a beautiful teapot from Kurdistan. I asked Andrew how he got it and he replied that it had been given to Prime Minister Tony Blair, whose wife didn't like it and somehow it made its way to Canon Andrew White's office. The teapot also came with cups and saucers which is very nice and it's far nicer drinking tea out of porcelain cup than out of a mug.

I loved his house as I used to be an antique dealer and I was simply in my element but also because there is something just so special about Canon Andrew White, he is unique and you would never find another character like Andrew's. I was truly amazed to think that Andrew's grandfather was once a plumber's assistant for the great charismatic preacher Smith Wigglesworth, one could understand why they were great people. Andrew also showed me his Smith Wigglesworth Bible that he had inherited, although it wasn't in good condition but when the Bible is well used, the devil is not amused.

I myself have a famous relative who was a missionary in the Solomon Islands in the 1930s, called John Seaton, who was a dentist and used to travel on horseback with a bottle of Whiskey to relieve the pain of his patients, many of which were cannibals, which is why it's amazing when we look into your genealogy.

Before I left, I was very honoured to be given a gift from Andrew of a wooden map of Iraq with a cross in the middle, carved by a gentleman who had not long passed away. I really treasured it but sadly, I lost it when I went to Kenya as a missionary which broke my heart.

Andrew's Office

Chapter 5
My Trip to Iraq

A few weeks later, I was asked to go to Erbil with the Kurdish family for six weeks and I was absolutely in awe of God at the way he had answered my prayer, "Is this all you have for my life?" I had been looking after the Chief Judge who had sentenced to death the leader of the Ba'ath Party, and President of Iraq. Not to mention the famous Vicar of Baghdad, Canon Andrew White. Therefore, I said yes, as it wasn't an opportunity to turn down and I had promised to make sure that I would return Mrs Raouf back to Mr Raouf safely. Who would have ever thought that Elaine would be asked to go to Iraq? In fact, I would never have thought I would have become best friends with the Chief Judge who sentenced Saddam. But I remember quite a few months ago that God had spoken to me in the night that he was taking me to the four corners of the Earth. In the morning, I dismissed it, thinking it must have been a dream but I could hear God saying, "Oh, ye of little faith."

After this time, everything seemed to go pear-shaped. The landlord decided to put the house I rented up for sale, and then there was a church split which caused me a lot of grief and heartache. I had also been praying a lot about my job that instead of having two part-time jobs, I would get a full-time position. However, after I went to the interview, I soon discovered that the management had given the job to someone else and the second time I applied, I didn't even get an interview. A part of me was devastated but obviously God knew the plans he had for my life, plans to prosper me and not to harm me but give me a hope and a future, and He had a better job for me lined-up.

I knew that God was up to something as He began to tell me to sell my goods and sort my finances out. Then before I knew it, I had handed in my notice for the rented house I was living in and my two jobs at The Elderfield. The strangest part of the story was that I had done all of this preparation before I knew I was going to be invited to Iraq by the Kurdish family I had helped. When God wants something to happen, nothing can stop His will, and He makes sure that you do things to help it happen.

I had no idea what to expect when I arrived in Iraq, other than what Brain had spoken about with his trips to see the Judge. He told me that the Kurdish family lived in a mansion surrounded by high walls, with barbed wire and helicopters going in and out. This gave me an indication that I would be very restricted as far as venturing out of his compound and I also knew that it would be extremely hot and dangerous for me as a Westerner. Arriving at the airport, I saw a well-dressed man who came up to the Kurdish family and lovingly kissed them and it turned out that this was their beloved son, with dark sunglasses which gave a presence of authority, and when your imagination runs wild, you could almost imagine you were in a scene from the Godfather.

When we arrived at their home, it was nothing like Brian had suggested. It was a normal house, very homely and comfortable, with armed guards outside for security but it certainly wasn't like Colditz Castle surrounded by barbed wire. 'Chee Chee' was Mr Raouf's maid and she was a lovely lady from the Philippines, who was employed to do the cooking, cleaning and the daily chores. I expect that she would send her wages home to look after her family or provide education for her children; yes, she was a lovely lady and I got on very well with her. I found that life in Erbil was very different to our lifestyle and culture in the UK and this was very much to do with extreme temperatures of 60–70° heat and therefore, they had to have a very different routine to ours. The family would get up very late and then rather than go shopping in the day time, they would go out from 11:00 pm onwards. One night, they took me to one of their huge shopping centres in the town and by 12:30 am, we were eating burgers at McDonald's whilst watching people ice skating; and by 1:30 am, we went to buy ice cream at an ice cream parlour. I had to chuckle as most mornings, you could find Mr Raouf sitting in his arm chair, reading a newspaper in pyjamas and a dressing gown. In fact, all the family members wore pyjamas or house coats to feel more comfortable in the heat of the day, that was their culture.

Breakfast consisted of bread, yogurt, cheese spread, eggs and peanut butter with some very sweet black Kurdish tea. The problem was that I wanted to lose weight and they had at least three meals a day, plus fruit and their famous Baklava cake, made out of filo pastry, with nuts and honey, for supper. I just envisaged myself getting fatter and fatter and fatter. One would have thought that during this time of Ramadan, my

Kurdish friends would be fasting, as they were Muslims with a faith in Allah, but they didn't fast because they said they were all suffering from illnesses. However, I did struggle with their entertainment as they would watch Al-Jazeera news and sometimes Korean movies or Muslim version of God TV all day and night, and it became quite boring as I didn't understand their language.

Some nights, my Kurdish friends would have guests come around to see Mr Raouf and his wife, and the men would sit in the far corner drinking tea and talking, laughing and planning whilst the women would chat on the sofa, wearing very smart dresses and head scarves as a covering. I remember one night I enjoyed Mr Raouf's granddaughter's birthday party whose parents had decorated the house with balloons and we had a great time blowing them up. Mr Raouf's daughter's sister and brother-in-law came to the party with their young son and he looked very handsome in his traditional Kurdish outfit and his wife who looked beautiful in her Kurdish attire. I must say they really know how to dress up and enjoy themselves. I even got to wear my beautiful purple evening dress with black lace frock and sequins as all the family looked smart and I didn't want to look out of place.

However, it was a bit strange to get dressed up for children's birthday parties because in England, we tend to go for jeans and a T-shirt. However, I did notice a few years later, when I went to a hotel in New City of Jerusalem that even in the Jewish culture, parents and children dress up at a Bar Mitzvah. However, I enjoyed engaging with all sorts of people and talking about their way of life and I liked their very beautiful and extravagant birthday cakes. It would have helped me if I had bought the right type of clothes with me so that it would suit their culture but I was thinking of six months in Kenya my destination after Iraq. Kurdish women would cover cleavage and arms, and wear a head scarf, whereas the clothes I had bought seemed to be the complete opposite. I seemed to have forgotten you can offend Muslim religious leaders in countries like Iraq and Saudi Arab by your attire or in their eyes lack of it.

In the past, you would have never, ever seen me in a Muslim home for several weeks, as the media portrays Muslims as being fanatics and evil people; although since becoming friends with the Kurdish family, I have come to respect Sunni and Sufi Muslims. They were very loving and hospitable people, who were treating me like royalty and their faith didn't really bother me as I knew who I was in Christ and wanted to convert them rather than the other way around. However at the end of my time in Iraq, we had mutual respect for each other's beliefs.

Mr Raouf loved his garden but hated the heat as it killed many of the flowers he had planted and watched grow. When he had a home in Halabja before Saddam gassed the community, he was well known for his beautiful garden with colourful flowers and so I gave him a 'Bird of Paradise Bulb' as it had a great significance to me, meaning the faithfulness of the groom to his bride which I saw as Yeshua.

To say thank you to Mr Raouf for all he had done for me, I bought him some Sapper beads which I believe touched his heart. Middle Eastern men use these beads all the time, counting the beads and praying. However, Mr Raouf was also very old-fashioned and liked everything to be done properly. I found this out to my peril as one day when I was just about to go with him to meet Abuna Andrew and Andrew's Iraqi adopted children, David and Lena, in a hotel in Ankawa. Ankawa used to be a small village until in 2014 when it received thousands of primarily Christian Refugees from Baghdad and Mosul but has grown into a city in its own right. Mr Raouf looked at me in a stern way and told me to change my dress, else he wouldn't take me, he would go on his own.

He wanted me to change as a matter of urgency, as he thought it was a night dress that I was wearing and he didn't want to look foolish, especially as we were having a meeting and lunch with Mr Lukman, the Iraqi Ambassador in UK, who I met before in London… He only had to look at you in a certain way and you knew you had to do as you were told. He didn't need to tell you twice…I must admit every time I think of that day, it did and does always make me chuckle.

A dress bought for me in Wallis, London.

A Kurdish dress bought for me in Erbil.

Mr Raouf's study became my bedroom and what an honour it was too. Even if I had to sleep on the floor, it would have been an honour, as I enjoyed looking through the Judge's books whilst rummaging among his drawers and boxes as I am a bit nosey, after all he is such an interesting man. How many other people would get to sleep in the study of the Chief Judge who sentenced Saddam Hussein? I spent a long time rummaging in hope of coming across the trial papers of Saddam or something as interesting but all I found were the Christian books he had been given by me and Brian, and books about Muslim faith. If I could have read Arabic, I would have been able to see what Judge Raouf had been writing about.

Mrs Raouf had worn a catheter on the plane because having had an operation on her leg, it would have been a rigmarole to have to go to the toilet; but now that she was home, she had an infection. This was a great worry to Mr Raouf but this was another chance to pray for them and once we had prayed for Jesus to heal her, she began to get a lot better and her family was much relieved; God was doing a great work on both of them.

Most days, I would be on my own until they all came back from work. I found being alone with only Muslim chants from Mecca and Iraqi National news about bombings and murders stressful, so I told Andrew and he told me to come to Baghdad where I could clean the clinic and help clean the new buildings for the school and visitors centre. So, I asked Mr Raouf and explained that Andrew had asked me to go to Baghdad. Can you imagine being firmly told by the Chief Judge who sentenced Saddam Hussein, "NO, YOU CAN'T GO TO BAGHDAD!!!!!!!"

Then I replied in tears, "But God said I have to go."

Mr Raouf's reply was, "If your God tells you to go to Baghdad, then you will have to go!!!"

At some point in the conversation, he even banged his fist on the table and I almost jumped out of my skin and ran up the stairs, throwing myself on the bed in tears. However, a very touching moment was when he begged me not to go to Baghdad, in fear I would never be seen again. He said he saw me like his daughter and he demanded that I didn't go as he loved me. What he said and the way he said it had me in more tears as no one had ever said that to me before and it meant so very much, but I had to go as God told me to go to Baghdad.

I hated having to tell him I was going to Baghdad because I really did respect him, as he was my host and it would have been a very controversial situation had I been arrested by the government or kidnapped whilst in Baghdad. I was oblivious to it all, to be honest; as if I hadn't been oblivious and naïve, I would have never gone out of Mr Raouf's front door. Mr Raouf's youngest daughter, had a dream that same night that there was a lot of confusion and Abuna (Father) Andrew just put me in the car and put bread around it or this white thing and I was fine.

Her family say her dreams come true and her premonition really did come to fruition as Andrew spoke to Mr Raouf and had been praying and talking to God. Maybe the bread that the youngest daughter saw was God's protection? However, her dream seemed to seal the deal and saw me going to Baghdad with Mr Raouf's permission, even though he didn't want me to go. There were great discussions how I was to go to Baghdad as they did speak of me going in a car and then being put in the car boot as I went over the Baghdad border. However Mr Raouf refused and in the end I went via plane which seemed less risky and more sensible.

I did like the youngest daughter, she is very practical, wise, funny and theatrical, and would make a very good film star, especially in Kurdistan. The eldest daughter is very elegant, calm and diplomatic but when it comes to her mum, she becomes very protective and sees to it that things get done for her. The middle daughter has a good sense of humour and as a lawyer, she can also be very determined and forceful, and doesn't mind a challenge. Mr Raouf junior is very loving towards his family, especially his mother, but he still looks like James Bond with his dark glasses and I got the sense that he knew how to look after himself and his family if need be. His wife is a doctor and works very hard, especially having to bring up a family. Mrs Raouf, who loves all her family, is my friend and even though we couldn't speak or talk the same language, you just know we are friends. Mr Raouf is a very special friend; he was like the father that I never had and I will always respect him and love him like my Kurdish Father.

I was very privileged to go and visit Mr Raouf at his office as Minister of Justice, in an armoured car with his youngest and oldest daughter who were his assistants. I not only sat in his daughter's office and watched them working but I also had the honour of having photos taken with the Minister of Justice in his court. However I never did get a copy of them or even see them. Although, who would have thought I would been living with these lovely people in the first place? It was all down to Andrew White's message on FB and his obedience to God.

Before I went to Baghdad, I picked up the Bible and God gave a verse that was to become like a rock that I had to believe and trust, as without Jesus and without faith, I couldn't continue with this journey and adventure.

Matthew 8 verses 23-27

23. Then he got into the boat and his disciples followed him.

24. Suddenly a furious storm came up on the lake, so that the waves swept over the boat. But Jesus was sleeping.

25. The disciples went and woke him, saying, "Lord, save us! We're going to drown!"

26. He replied, "You of little faith, why are you so afraid?" Then he got up and rebuked the winds and the waves, and it was completely calm.

27. The men were amazed and asked, "What kind of man is this? Even the winds and the waves obey him!"

After reading the verses, I realised that God was going to have me walk on water.

Chapter 6
Baghdad

I was sat on the plane heading for Baghdad now that Andrew had squared my journey at the reception with Ali. This was very worrying for Mr Raouf because everyone seemed to be called Ali in Baghdad and he said everyone in Baghdad was called Ali, so how would I know who the right one was?

I must admit, I was in fear and trembling because I had an Israeli stamp on my passport, made worse by the fact that Mr Raouf had warned me about what could happen if I was arrested by the Iraq Government, as I would never be seen again. Also the realities of Baghdad. He told me that if I was arrested by the government, I would never be seen again and he couldn't help me. On the other hand, I was worried I would be kidnapped by Al Qaeda but I knew that it was God's will for me to go to Baghdad and I trusted Andrew as he was so close to God with a special anointing.

Sitting on the plane to Baghdad, I was very frightened, with my mind full of scenarios of what might happen once I arrived in Baghdad and prayed verbally and inwardly for God's help. In front of me were two Arab looking men and I overheard them talking about Christians, rockets and missiles which caused me to think they were perhaps suicide bombers or wanted to hijack the plane. So, what did I do? I prayed some more, I prayed for forgiveness and I also prayed over the land and I asked for the joy of the Lord to be my strength and repeatedly said the Lord's Prayer, in case I was going to be blown up out of the sky.

I just kept saying, "Our Father, who art in heaven," quite loudly and people looked at me very strangely, wondering who I was and what I was doing on the plane to Baghdad. However, I arrived on Baghdad soil in one piece, seemingly safe, alive and well but very frightened, like a rabbit in the middle of the road looking at on-coming traffic with beams of light in the night.

As I got off the plane, I saw a car drive past and I thought this was it, I was going to be arrested by the government and locked in a prison cell for the rest of my life or I was going to die through gruesome torture. However, before long, I was in the airport heading for the visa department and walked into my worst nightmare. I had been told by Andrew that Ali, the "Mr Fix it", in the visa section was going to be there and that he and Lukman had sorted everything out and there would be no problem getting me a visa, so that I could go straight through immigration and Andrew would be waiting for me on the other side. This was not the case, as there was no Andrew and no Ali.

When I gathered up my confidence and asked if Ali had any information about my Visa to get into Baghdad, they had no idea what I was talking about or who the Ali was? The song 'Alice' came rushing to mind and I had to laugh. Thankfully, an American lady came to the rescue and let me borrow her phone because mine had run out of battery. I managed to get through to Andrew who told me to stay where I was as he was on his way. Thank God, a policeman came up to me and asked if I was Elaine who was special? I knew then Andrew had already started to sort things but what came into my mind was that special could have been interpreted as something to be frightened of, cuffed to a bench, being tortured. In the meantime, I had an embarrassing moment, as when I went to sit on a chair to wait for Andrew in the Visa Department, it tipped up, which had everybody in a fit of laughter.

This must have broken the ice because as I got up, they offered me food as it was the end of Ramadan and I even got a marriage proposal which was so amusing. It was quite a relief that these guys were really kind and had great sense of humour, not the barbaric men I had imagined.

Everyone was still laughing at my request to see Ali as they were all called Ali, just as Mr Raouf had stated, even he wanted to know who Ali was before I left for the plane, indeed everyone wanted to know who Ali was and I don't think I ever did meet Ali. Andrew arrived sometime later in the evening which just got more amusing by the minute and the joy of the Lord filled the place. Andrew phoned Lukman, the Iraqi Ambassador in London, to try and get me a visa, as at that point, I hadn't got one. In the end, Andrew went to the organ grinder, General Yasin, who spoke to the head of the Visa department and I got one without any problem.

Because of all the negative conversations I had about coming to Baghdad, I actually deleted all the photos of the Kurdish family for security reasons, as I didn't want them to know I was staying with the minister of justice. However, Andrew told the world and his wife about where Elaine had been and whom she was staying with. Rather than be arrested, they just laughed and maybe like everyone else who didn't believe my story, they too simply didn't believe what was said was true? They probably laughed, thinking it was a joke? Who knows? It certainly wasn't as bad as I had thought it would be, in Baghdad Airport; in fact, I was glad I hadn't been arrested and I was still alive. God knew what he was doing because arriving late in the evening, the Visa Department had more time to deal with my problem; whereas in the morning, they would have been very busy and I would have had to wait a very long time to get this all sorted out. This is why it's all about God's timing and that's perfect. After going through Airport Control and collecting my bag, I went with Canon Andrew White to the car and met Lena Andrew's PA, who had stayed with their driver, Abusena.

I wasn't sure what Baghdad would look like but whilst Erbil was a glorified building site, Baghdad was very much like a crumbling old city originated from continuous bombing. However, in the dark, it was very difficult to see anything but I was so tired, I just wanted to go to sleep. The church itself was very beautiful, as was the room that I had been given, much better than what I had expected. I had envisaged living in a very small room, like a tin can, but it even had a fridge with some food inside and drinks; it was lovely and a great surprise. I was so delighted to be in Baghdad alive and safe and for that one night, I didn't worry about bombs and killings, I just went straight to sleep.

It was the Kurdish tradition to walk around in their bed clothes until someone came around or they went out because it is so very hot, but now in Baghdad, no more pyjama parties, it was now down to work and getting up very early whilst it wasn't as hot. Abusena brought me two fried eggs, some flat bread and a cup of tea, which was very welcome and tasty, and that's what I had for breakfast for the next three weeks. I really was treated like a queen, having everything done for me and I felt so guilty, really guilty because back in the UK, I normally do everything myself. Even the Kurdish family treated me like a queen and I felt so honoured and yet so guilty because serving others is my heart.

Abusena was Andrew's Muslim driver and in a place like Baghdad, some people may have had trust issues because of the nature of Andrew's work and the political climate, but I didn't get involved with politics whilst I was there. However, Andrew was a discerning man and very wise because with all the check points and security issues, it was far better to have a local driver who knew people and the roads. I did like Abusena, he was very funny yet hard working and he made me two fried eggs and a cup of tea most mornings; then on another occasion, he made me the most delicious omelette I have ever tasted.

Another man who I met in St George's was Edward, who was the Christian Caretaker, he didn't look like how I imagined an Iraqi to be; he was fair-haired, not like the dark swarthy skin which generally Arabs seem to have. Edward lived on the compound with his wife and three children as he needed a safe haven from death threats from terrorists.

During the Iraq war with Iran, Edward became a Prisoner of War, for fourteen years and it was during this time, he became a Christian. At the same time, he discovered that one of his Lieutenants was a spy for Iran, who had trapped his own troops, so the Iranians could shoot them, pull their eyes out and slit their throats, and they actually crucified one soldier. During the war, he was shot in the side and taken to hospital where an Iranian put his fingers in the wound very harshly as a form of torture but Edward punched the soldier and managed to escape, despite being in tremendous pain.

Edward had been through so much in Iraq because even as a bodyguard for the USA in Baghdad, he had witnessed suicide bombings and many people being killed. Yet he and his family now serve St George's, doing many jobs; and in doing so, serve the LORD in the hope that one day they will go and live in another country away from the terror of living in Baghdad.

On my first day in Baghdad, I went to St Theresa's Home with Andrew, the Vicar of Baghdad and Lena, Andrew's PA, Lena, in their blacked-out car driven by Abusena. It was quite exciting sitting in a car in between two security pickup trucks, with armed guards carrying guns. I suppose having lived and worked in Belfast kind of softened its impact.

Driving in the daylight enabled me to see what it was really like in Baghdad and my first impression was that it actually wasn't as bad as I was led to believe. I thought it would look like a building site because of all the bombing, yet it looked no different to any other Middle East Country that I have been to, such as Tunisia and Turkey.

When we arrived at the Catholic Children's home, we were greeted by St Teresa's Nuns and a couple of children, one girl with no limbs, one boy Yasin who had Cerebral Palsy was a lovely child. Having been married to Nigel with Muscular Dystrophy and having looked after my son who had Hirschsprung's disease, disability didn't faze me; therefore, seeing children with no limbs or with Cerebral Palsy and Spinal Bifida wasn't a problem for me. All I felt was love for these children who were in this sorry state, stricken with disease and mental and physical disabilities because of chemical warfare which affected them during their time in their mother's womb. Many children with disabilities are left at the roadside to die, abandoned by their parents, because they are seen as a curse when they are indeed a blessing.

If I'd had the finances, I would have offered to have adopted Yasin or at least I could have invested in his education because despite his disability, he had great character and was a very bright child. Like the other children, had he had the opportunity, he would go far in life. However being in an Orphanage in Baghdad, his chances were limited. Andrew took me back to see Yasin the following week and this time Andrew and his team fed the boys and girls who needed help. A little girl who was severely disabled crawled quite quickly across the floor, like a crab, and kept taking Andrew's glasses off his face which made everyone giggle; he is so good with these children.

One day, Lena found a link to YouTube where a young man called Emmanuel, a contestant in the Australian X Factor, told his amazing story of how he and his brother, Ahmed, both limbless, were brought up in St Theresa's Orphan School, Baghdad, and were adopted by an Australian woman. She took them back to Australia where they had successful operations to help give them a better quality of life and provided both boys with education. Now Emmanuel has the chance of a lifetime especially if he won the singing competition. At the same time his brother is the fastest swimmer in the world, and was in the Paralympics. Andrew, of course, knew this story well and also the woman who adopted the two boys.

We can see in this miraculous story how the Lord doesn't forsake his children. He gives them a hope and a future, so we are praying Yasin will get similar opportunities.

On another occasion, we went to an American Army Camp to pick up some things from a general whom Andrew knows really well. However, we didn't get very far as Abusena's Green Zone pass had run out and the General hadn't given out the necessary paperwork. Andrew was very frustrated and so whilst he and his driver waited in the car, Lena and I walked up and down to find how we could get a pass on site, but in the end, we were told to leave by an NCO because Abusena was parked in his car space and we had no passes.

Andrew was far from pleased and so the following day, he emailed the General and told him quite frankly what a palaver it was just to go and pick up a few items that the General himself had asked Andrew to collect. Andrew did say that when the US eventually leave, it was going to be chaos in Baghdad because Iraqi soldiers will struggle. These turned out to be very prophetic words, as in 2015, we saw just that with ISIS trying to take over Iraq and on the verge of marching to Baghdad, beheading men, women, children, raping women and killing anyone who was a Christian.

The first night I had arrived in Baghdad, I wasn't scared, just so glad to have arrived in one piece, but the following night when I went to bed, I was feeling rather frightened on my own in the bedroom. I had night terrors, worried that the Al Qaeda would break in the Church and kidnap me. If Andrew had been a woman, I would have asked to have slept on the floor in his bedroom; even with the mice, lizards and ants on the floor, I would have felt safer. However, I did pray to the Lord to help me and also asked Facebook friends to pray for me too. I woke up feeling the joy of the Lord but that was short-lived as there had been a number of bomb attacks in Baghdad and so maybe this was God telling me to pray rather than moan?

After a few days of settling in, I began to clean the windows and floors of the new building for the school and the Visitors' Quarters. My train of thought was to clean each room one at a time, first the windows, then the floor, and get rid of paint splashes with a scrubbing brush. I asked Edward for a scraper and used a little water to scrape the paint off, which is why it took hours and hours, leaving my hands and nails very sore.

You had to remember this was Iraq, not the UK, there was more paint on the floor than the ceiling and walls, also varnish was all over the place. Even the windows were covered with cement, which is why it would have been a lot easier to put a cover on the floor and do the dirtiest jobs first. I know the windows wanted cleaning outside but even with armed guards, I still worried about being shot or kidnapped. I knew I was overreacting but it wasn't until I got used to being in St George's Church that I could stand outside and clean them. In the meantime, the cavalry arrived in Iraqi time, as women and children came with a water hose and long sweepers to clean the floor three hours too late.

They used so much water to swill down the floors that it was actually like a swimming pool and water was everywhere, including the new doors, and yet the workers were really happy with their work. At one stage, they poured gasoline on the floor and used it to clean off the paint and varnish stuck to the tiles. I just looked and thought to myself that all it will take is a person to light up a cigarette, and drop the match on the floor and the whole place would go up and it wouldn't be an act of terrorism but rather stupidity!

Elaine cleaning paint off of the floor in the new
St George's visitors' area

Rather than lose my temper, I just thought we have to do as the Romans do and change is a process, also I didn't want to appear interfering or seen as taking over. Actually, I had loads of fun and laughter working with the ladies and I bonded really well with the girls and I was really honoured because one lady gave me an Iraqi 'friends' bracelet and the other a ring. In the end, I realised that rather than be a perfectionist, I should simply engage with the girls and get to know them and it made more of an impact on our work performance, and in the end, the rooms looked very beautiful. The following day, instead of helping clear the floor, because Father Fiaz was going to use a professional floor cleaner to get all the paint and cement off the tiles, I ended up cleaning the pharmacy, sorting out the pills and medicines, getting them in date order and wiping off the dust that had accumulated.

I really enjoyed this as it reminded me of when I worked in Kelly's chemist in the Falls Road, Belfast, as a young teenager in the late 70s, as even there, we were always worried about terrorism. However, just like here in Baghdad, you just got on with it. I enjoyed living and working among the Iraqi people, who sat on the floor to eat a big banquet of food, as it was great fun and I enjoyed the stuffed vine leaves and aromatic rice. I also enjoyed sitting down and all holding hands and praying for them. One single lady, who I got on well with, told me that she was a lecturer in engineering but she was still single because she was looking after her parents and we sort of struck a chord. She was also friends with a lady who I got in with in St George's gift shop.

The Workers' Lunch

The lady in the shop told me her tragic story of how her son had been murdered by terrorists five years ago and she has been in mourning ever since. She showed me a picture of her son in his coffin after he had been tortured. But despite the terrible injuries to his face, he was beautiful and he looked like he had just seen Yeshua/ Jesus. The radiance of Christ on his face reminded me of Nigel after he died as if he had met with the Lord, they both had a glow that was angelic, which is why I wasn't at all fazed by this. All I thought was that it's now time to stop mourning and it's time to live, although you can never forget the person or what happened but we do need to forgive as Christ forgives us.

The other sad story was that the Iraqi man and his Christian family, who were cleaners in St George's, once owned a shop and sold alcohol and because of this, his two children had their brains blown out by terrorists. The man showed me the photos of his children and they made me feel so sad at the loss of two young people's lives. He himself had his leg blown off in war and thanks to Abuna Andrew, he was able to have a new artificial leg. Such a kind act meant that this man can now walk and live a far more normal life than before and he can work for a wage and that gives him satisfaction in life.

Despite all people's suffering and tragic loss, the joy of the Lord is in St George's Church because as it says in Psalms 30:11-12 that the Lord turns our ashes into beauty, and sorrow into joy, and mourning into dancing, and that's exactly what the Lord is doing. Outside the church is war and inside is God's peace, the peace that the world doesn't know and passes all understanding.

One day, Andrew went to find the grave of Gertrude Bell in a local graveyard. Although she was an archaeologist, Gertrude Bell was seen as the British instigator of Iraq as it is today. Gertrude set up Iraqi boundary perimeters in Saudi Arabia, Iran and Turkey etc. as she got involved with politics. Gertrude was a very prominent lady as she combined her expertise and her archaeology with political influence… She would have been seen as the Andrew White of her day.

However, on another occasion, I had the privilege to go with Lena and Andrew to another graveyard to find a high-ranking officer's grave who died in 1920s (I think it was General Weldon). Andrew was doing this on behalf of the Weldon family as the grave is in Andrew's parish. Unlike the average vicar in UK, Andrew has to take security with him wherever he goes in Baghdad and even when Andrew is looking for a war grave, his security has to come too.

We all got out of the car and began to search for a grave with General Weldon written on it, even though they were covered with weeds and prickly plants can be a hiding place for snakes. At one point, we heard gun fire in the distance and we realised that we were the target yet we were all determined to find the right grave and to be honest, at the time, we feared the snakes rather than the terrorists, who were just a nuisance, just as the dates were hard to find on the graves, 1916–1918. But alas, it was impossible to continue in the heat and with the very high prickly weeds and with people shooting at us all around and we decided to go back on another day.

A Graveyard in Baghdad

A little later whilst driving through the green zone, they took me to see the cross swords of Saddam Hussein. They were made by an English man out of the Iranian planes shot down during the Iraq/Iran war. The helmets of Iranian soldiers killed by the Iraq soldiers were at the bottom of the cross swords. The funny thing was that the wife of the English man who made this monument lives in the same warden-controlled home as Andrew's mum, Pauline; that's so ironic.

Crossed Swords in Baghdad

The base of the Crossed Swords made from the helmets of Iranian prisoners of war

On another occasion, I was standing under the cross swords in the heart of Baghdad with Daniel, the very man who Andrew spoke about in Leicester University. He was the son of a Shiite tribal leader in Baghdad and after Daniel had come to faith in a US prison, he was one of the eleven men that Andrew baptised. Daniel shared with me that he had asked the

US prison guards to get him a Bible as he wanted to study the topic of Abraham and once he began to read about Yeshua the Messiah, and his teachings, he began to see that the Bible made more sense than the Koran.

He explained that Koran portrayed Isa (Jesus) as a prophet rather than the Messiah, and that he converted to Christianity. Being a convert to Christianity, he couldn't tell his father or his wife of his new found faith in fear of being murdered. However, the Lord met with him in such a way that Daniel explained he couldn't and wouldn't give up his faith.

Daniel also shared with us that the Lord had been working on his father, as one day a Christian man living in Baghdad was having terrible problems with his Muslim neighbours and in desperation, the Christian decided to go and visit Daniel's father for advice. Obviously, this put the Christian man in danger as Daniel's father was the leader of the Shiite tribe but this was the Christian man's only option. After taking the bull by the horns, the Christian man spoke for a long time with Daniel's father and Daniel believes that God gave his father great wisdom in this situation as he came up with a very clever solution.

He explained to the Muslims that the Christian was a man of faith and didn't cause his people any problems and he would never upset anybody, therefore, if they hurt him, they shouldn't come running complaining to him; however, if the Christian man had been a trouble maker, he would have sorted the problem out himself. The Christian was so grateful to the tribal leader that he gave him a Bible because the Bible meant the most to him and was all that he had. Daniel's father was so touched by the Christian man's gesture, that he himself began to read the Bible and just as Daniel found, the Bible made more sense to him than the Koran and he acknowledged that the Bible is full of wisdom.

Just like his father, Daniel said he is often called to sort out problems and on one occasion, he was called to sort out a case of adultery but rather than get the tribe together to stone the woman to death, he prayed to God to ask him what he should do. Daniel felt that God wanted him to help the woman and heard God saying, he without sin cast the first stone. Daniel was so impressed by God's advice that he put the onus on the man rather than the woman and made the man pay his tribe a lot of money whilst telling the man to leave his home for a whole year after making sure his tribe and the woman agreed to this first. Daniel said many times women are raped and are then blamed and accused of being the one to have caused the situation, rather than being seen as the man's fault. God, through his grace and mercy, really helped Daniel to solve a difficult problem which helped him to look right in the eyes of his tribe, who knew nothing about his salvation and his life was now right before God.

I saw Daniel again at St George's when he came with us to the US Embassy's Sunday service and I must say that he looked very powerful and prominent in his Sheikh's attire, he wore a long white robe and a Keffiyeh Arabic head dress worn in the Middle East. I was quite taken aback by his presence of authority and realised how difficult it must be for him being, both a son of a local tribal leader and a born-again Christian, as he was so restricted, not being able to worship God openly in fear of being murdered. I sympathised with Daniel because it was tough for me not being able to leave the compound on my own; as being a white Christian woman, I would have been kidnapped and held for ransom, so how much worse it was for Daniel in his own community.

One night, when we were driving back to St George's, we had hoped to drive through the green zone. However, when one of the guards asked Lena to give him her phone, she refused and after an exchange of angry words, the guard refused us entry; therefore, Abusena had to turn around and drive back along the unprotected roads in Baghdad. I was so frightened that I put a scarf over my head, trying to reduce exposing my white face and blond hair. I was also frightened that we would pass a suicide bomber or get shot at by terrorists, yet praise God, we arrived in St George's in one piece because the hand of God was with us. However, the experience really showed me what these people have to face and go through day after day, after day, running the gauntlet of suicide bombers and terror attacks, which is why I really appreciated what Canon Andrew White must have gone through as the Vicar of Baghdad, living most of the time in Baghdad with a massive price on his head.

On another occasion, Andrew took me and Lena to Baghdad Central to buy a carpet and a picture for the visitors lounge in St George's. To my sheer horror, Andrew asked me to come with him and Lena into the shop. I felt really insecure and worried as I got out of the car; in fact, I felt sheer panic, even though we had armed security as they wouldn't have stopped us from being blown up. We spent ages and ages in the shop and I just wanted to get back in the car and go back to St George's, although being in the car alone would have been even more risky. After a long time of haggling and deciding, Andrew chose a Picture which could easily pass as

Bible character Abraham for his new visitors lounge and then thankfully, we went on our merry way.

The Picture Andrew bought of Abraham
for the new Guest House

One of the nicest days I experienced in Baghdad was when I went to the American Embassy which once was one of Saddam's Palaces, to see Hank Bond becoming a US Admiral in the US Navy. I also met many US Generals and Colonels who were Christians and I even got to sit in Saddam's chair. This was followed by a visit to the Australian Embassy for lunch and it was like a scene out of a James Bond film, as one man was wearing an expensive suit and held a machine gun covered with a beautiful linen cloth. I also got into conversation with Deputy Ambassador David Livingstone, who I got on very well with, as he was so charming and diplomatic. However, I was rather shocked as he wore two earrings in his ear and I did wonder if he had been a hippy in his youth?

Saddam's palace   Elaine sitting on Saddam's throne

Elaine with Admiral Hank Bond   Me with Deputy Ambassador Mr Livingstone

I really enjoyed chatting with Andrew at night, putting the world to rights and talking about our faith and being Christians on the front line. We both had similar childhoods and had gone through a lot of life experiences and as Andrew was such an interesting person with lots of stories to tell, you never got bored with his company. I saw Andrew like the brother I never had and he had a deep understanding of people through his own suffering, although I wouldn't like to cross him as I wouldn't Mr Raouf because they were both powerful characters.

One evening as we sat eating supper and drinking juice, I was fascinated to learn that whilst Andrew was training to be a prison chaplain, he had to spend a month in a prison as a part of his training to get a greater understanding of prison life as an offender. The prisoners thought he was a homosexual and therefore they were constantly trying to verbally abuse Andrew and pick a fight with him. However, as he ran the gauntlet and passed several cells, the prisoners saw that he could handle himself by giving as good as they gave him and once they found out he was the new chaplain, he won their respect.

During the first week of my three-week stay in Baghdad, Andrew and Lena went to a Peace and Reconciliation Conference in Lebanon and I was left on my own for a few days. I really enjoyed cooking for the Priest and the caretaker's family in the day time, but that night I felt very isolated and in great fear that terrorists might come and kidnap me to torture me to death. That was always my biggest fear and so rather than sleep in my room, I spent the night in Andrew's bed with my head under the covers, eating his sweets, as I felt peace there and the presence of the Lord because Andrew was a very anointed man of God. There were armed Christian guards and security all around the compound at St George's and even outside the room but I also knew God's protection and believed in His Word. All Jesus kept telling me was, "Where is your faith? I am here." This is what I felt at the time when I was in Baghdad and God kept showing me the verses about the disciples screaming for Jesus to wake up to stop the storm, but Jesus asked the disciples where was their faith? I even found an old poster of that very verse in my room. However, I was truly relieved when Andrew and Lena returned back to St George's Church and his anointing came back with him!

I loved the choir, they sang like angels, and one Sunday, I sang a song in Arabic with the choir and they sang an English song with me, called 'In the glory of your presence'. I also went to choir practice as they had a massive task ahead of them, having to sing a hymn that is sung in English, in Saint Paul's Cathedral, to the Bishop who was coming to commission Fiaz as a deacon. I knew that they would sing the hymn well but they needed to roll their *R*'s to make it sound more realistic, as their accent would make it hard for others to understand what they were singing about. We all prayed that God would really help them on that Sunday to sound like angels. We also prayed for Hanni and his wife, whom I loved dearly, that she would conceive as they really wanted a baby, which she did a year or so later.

The Mothers' Union were amazing too as they would visit Christian and Muslim families, who were often very poor and in dire need. They told me that once they visited a woman in hospital and her baby had just died and so they prayed the baby would be raised from the dead and this is exactly what happened because as soon as they had prayed, the baby began to cry. What joy the mum and the members of the Mothers' Union must have felt and every one was crying tears of great joy and happiness at God's miracle. One Sunday, after the service where I had just given a talk, I was asked to distribute food out to both Muslim and Christian church members and it was such a real privilege. Thank you, Lord, for meeting such wonderful people and providing for their precious needs.

Chapter 7
Halabja

When going back to Kurdistan, I was supposed to check my luggage in at Baghdad Departure Lounge, and then meet Andrew and Lena in the arrival area but when I tried to get through into Arrivals, the guard said that I had to go over the bridge and back to the Departure Lounge. However, I simply didn't want to go up a flight of stairs on my own, especially as I was absolutely terrified of being kidnapped. I was so frightened that I began to hyperventilate and I couldn't breathe, especially travelling alone, I was just a sitting target. I was really in fear of my life, anybody could come and abduct me, especially after hearing from other people that the terrorists are ignored by the police and army due to fear. I almost passed out with extreme heat and how I got to the army checkpoint where you had to have your case searched, I really don't know. I was absolutely terrified and quaking in my boots, until I got to the departure lounge and by that time, I couldn't stop coughing. I have never been in such a state of sheer fear and panic in all of my life.

Before I went to Baghdad, I wasn't scared at all, I was more intrigued; but after listening to people's stories of how their loved ones had been kidnapped and tortured, I was quite traumatised and left feeling fearful. A case of what you don't know and see, but when you do see the realities of life in Baghdad, it's a different ball game.

I didn't miss not meeting the Bishop as I was just so pleased to be alive and in one piece. It wasn't that I was a coward but after all that I had heard and seen, mixed up with imagination, I can't express just how scared I was. Scared of the unknown and terrors of the evil one. I thought, *Elaine, stop this, just trust in the Lord as he is your protection; but you can't help looking around, asking yourself if this person in the car is Al Qaeda terrorist? Is this car a taxi or is it going to come and drive past me and kidnap me?* It was ridiculous really as the security in the airport was very tight but being alone caused me to feel vulnerable.

I waited in the Airport for several hours and then I finally got on the plane; however, despite the trauma, I did cry as we took off from Baghdad, having truly enjoyed my time there as it was the exact opposite of what I had expected. I have never met such hospitable people in all of my life. I was never once treated badly. They couldn't do enough for me and I also went to places and met people I never ever thought I would. I met admirals in the US Navy and Army, government officials and tribal leaders. I also thanked God and Canon Andrew White as very few people ever come to Baghdad and even fewer get to sit in Saddam's chair, never mind stay with the family of the judge who sentenced Saddam Hussein. Also many people have visited Baghdad and have never been heard of again.

When I arrived in the airport, I was wondering where Mr Raouf's daughter was? I had expected to have gone straight through security, like we had before when I first arrived in Erbil, being a guest of Mr Raouf, Minister of Justice, however, I had to go through the ordinary security with the other passengers. Once through, Mr Raouf's daughter rang me, asking where I was as she was waiting for me in the arrivals' lounge in the Airport. I explained I was in the airport arrivals' lounge also but I couldn't see her, neither of us could see each other, that's when the penny dropped that I was in the wrong airport. I couldn't believe that I was, in fact, in Sulaymaniyah and not Erbil, and wondered what I was going to do.

The problem was that normally the plane goes from Baghdad to Sulaymaniyah and then to Erbil but this time the plane's first stop was Erbil and as I couldn't understand Arabic, I continued with the flight. In fact, I hadn't a clue that I was at the wrong destination until my Kurdish friend rang me, who I later found out had been who had been ringing me for hours. However, God saved the day as her cousins who had travelled with us from UK were staying with their aunties in Sulaymaniyah and Mr Raouf's daughter arranged for me to stay with them for a few days.

When looking back, I believe that this wasn't an accident but God had sent me to Sulaymaniyah to enable me to visit Halabja to pray over the land and meet more of the Kurdish family. Halabja is a place I had always wanted to visit even more so now as it's here that Mr Raouf's lovely family and friends once lived before the war, and escaped to Iran at the time of the chemical bombing on March 16th, 1988. The bombing of mass destruction caused between 3,200–5,000 deaths, injuring up to 10,000 people, causing both diseases and birth defects. It was largest chemical weapon attack on any civilisation and it was truly catastrophic and a miracle that Mr Raouf's family had escaped.

Halabja was now just a very dusty village in the middle of Barren land, everywhere looked derelict, although it didn't help because it was a Friday, a Holy Day, for Muslims just like Sundays are for Christians. As we were walking to where Mr Raouf used to live my friends remembered their Grandfather who hid in bunker downstairs and put damp cloth in every crevice or place where gas could get in, to soak it up. They also recalled their escape to Iran until it was safe to return. On arriving to the site where Mr Raouf's home was once situated, the family recalled how in its heyday the house would have had a beautiful garden with many sweet-smelling flowers, why it truly was a very sad moment. We visited the Halabja museum where they commemorate that terrible day when Saddam sent weapons of mass destruction to annihilate the Kurdish people of Halabja. We saw endless photos of children with their faces swollen and blood coming from their mouths and all the dead had huge blisters on their body. It was so horrific, it looked like something from an X-rated horror movie, you couldn't help but get emotional. It has the same effect on the Kurds as the Holocaust has on the Jewish people.

Some people escaped to Iran, like the Raouf family, whilst many suffered terrible deaths, whilst on their way to make a new life in Iran having suffered with radiation sickness. One of the most traumatic photos for me was to see their bodies shovelled on a cart and thrown into huge mass graves as if their lives simply didn't matter. However, after this trip, I knew that God did care as Mr Raouf was given the job to sentence Saddam Hussein who was responsible for killing many of his family and community. This is why I stood at the top high point of Halabja and prayed over the land repenting for this terrible act of genocide. I also prayed God's forgiveness on behalf of Saddam Hussein and his men for what they did. It says in the Bible that God turns ashes into beauty, sorrow into joy and mourning into dancing, why I believe the way forward is that we work for peace not endless killing. Why we must not forget what happened on the 16th March 1988 when a whole community died a terrible death.

This was for me a journey of a lifetime, even though I had been to one of the most unpopular and most dangerous places on Earth. However, God had taken me to Iraq to pray for the salvation of Mr Raouf and his family then to Halabja to pray and repent on behalf of Saddam Hussein for the Halabja mass genocide where 5,000 Kurds were killed and 100,000 injured though chemical warfare. God also took me to Baghdad where I met Daniel under the Crossed Swords, the very same son of a Shiite who Andrew spoke about in 2009 during his talk at Leicester University.

I never thought I would ever visit such a place and meet such wonderful people as it is here I learned not to take care but take risks. What an amazing time I had had and what awesome men and women I met along the way including Canon Andrew White, one of the most important yet underestimated and underrated man of the 21st century for such a time as this and he deserves to have an MBE, OBE and a Knighthood for 'not taking care but taking risks', so that people's lives, especially children were made bearable and loved and kept from the hands of terrorists.

Father Fiaz of St Georges Church Baghdad.
Standing next to the wax work of Saddam Hussein, in Madam Tussauds Museum London.

Once the six weeks visit to Iraq had come to an end, I became a missionary for four years in Kenya which was the other part of God's plan and purpose for my life; however, I still helped Andrew once or twice when I came home on furlough. On one occasion, I had the great privilege to be able to host Deacon Fiaz and his wife on a trip to London with Andrew's PA Lena, when they came to England for a long-awaited visit and it was nice to see them again. We met in Petersfield and then travelled to London by train which was a great experience for the couple from war-torn Baghdad. They loved the spectacular views from the London eye and visiting Madame Tussauds's Wax Work Museum, where we took a photo of Father Fiaz standing next to a wax work of Saddam Hussein. It was quiet a day out for the Iraqi couple, and we did have a great time and enjoyed a lovely lunch in an old London pub opposite St Thomas Hospital where Andrew trained as a 'Gasman' or should I say an Anaesthetist.

I think Father Fiaz and his wife were very overwhelmed by the change of environment from the bombed city of Baghdad, to our vibrant capital city. London was brimming with people of different cultures, faiths and historical background, who freely went about just doing their own thing, without bombs going off daily and people fearing they would get killed by a suicide bomber. There was simply so much to see and do, in such a short space of time, and I had to laugh as even the rain seemed to be something new for the Iraqi couple living in such a very hot country.

On another occasion, I met Father Fiaz and his wife in Winchester who were taking part in a combined Mothers' Union Service on behalf of their members in St George's with the members of Winchester Cathedral. The Cathedral is a very splendid building with beautiful stained-glass windows and architecture that dated back hundreds of years full of pomp, ceremony and history. During the service, I saw a glimpse of Gehad who escorted the couple on this trip but I didn't get chance to speak to him as I had to leave early to visit my friends at Langley House Trust but it was wonderful to have the opportunity to have met Father Fiaz and his wife again and also Lena.

Sadly, since this time ISIS terrorist group has killed and tortured many Iraqi Christians, including children and adults who attended St George's, as they wouldn't denounce their faith in Yeshua/ Jesus/Isa. Whilst many Iraqi Christians fled places like Nineveh for safety but, in fact, they fled to their deaths as Isis conquered Nineveh and slaughtered hundreds if not thousands of Christian. However, some of Andrew's children are now refugees in a school in Jordan, supported and run by Andrew and his Charity, Jerusalem Merit. Some of

Andrew's adult congregation managed to flee to USA and Canada.

During my time in Kenya, I would go on Facebook to keep in contact with friends and one day, I saw a post saying that Mr Raouf had been murdered by ISIS in retaliation for Saddam's execution. I was so shocked and truly very upset that I cried for many hours, as my heart was filled with great sadness. I was simply devastated by this news. Thankfully, after posting all my woes and pain on Facebook of the death of Mr Raouf, a wonderful friend messaged me to say that he had found out, (to my joy,) that it was a LIE! FAKE NEWS. Mr Raouf was still alive, so I jumped, up and down with great joy as I love Mr Raouf and his family dearly. I will never forget their kindness towards me, that's why I remain friends with the family today. It really didn't matter that they are Sunni Muslim and I am Christian. What did matter was being able to share love and respect for each other even in times of difficulties and trials.

Looking back now, I can understand why Mr Raouf was upset and worried, about my trip to Baghdad, because he was my host, and if anything had have happened to me that was untoward then it would have put his life in danger and cause a tremendous controversy for him and his family. Canon Andrew White could have also been in terrible trouble but if we didn't 'Take Risks', we would never experienced the wonderful power of the Lord and His presence, meet people you would never meet and do things you would never do. I just can't believe what God has done for me and how he answered my prayer, "I*s this all you have for my life?"* but do you know what? I am so very glad he did! Amen…

Chapter 8
A New Beginning

The next part of God's plan came in a very unexpected way. Having lived in a mud hut for several years in Kenya after I had left Iraq, I prayed for a husband, because of loneliness. Then of the blue, God told me that I needed to get accountability for my work in Kenya as a Missionary. I emailed my friend Bishop Andrew Hall, from Glasgow for his advice who told me to email Bishop Adrian who was the Bishop of the Cross Denominational Mission and Bishop of the Old Catholic Apostolic Church Worldwide. This I did and Mr Trimlett Glover sent me a certificate that stated I was their Missionary in Kenya. Amazingly when I came back on to UK on furlough, he asked if he could ring me and I realised he wanted to make sure I was a real person and not a Facebook scammer.

Once I had returned to West End Southampton, to stay with a friend, we arranged to meet up in my friend's farmhouse to chat about Missionary work and Church. After Bishop Adrian had had a cup of tea, and came to the realisation that I was a genuine person and a real missionary, he asked if he could take me to a church where we could pray.

We drove around for quite a time as most churches nearby were closed but we ended up in Hedge End, Anglican Church, where we spent time in prayer and singing from a hymn book. Before I knew it, we hugged and I will never forget it as I felt like God had hugged me. I didn't want it to end as I had had no real affection in four years. Adrian had a real anointing and when he prayed, you could quite see his authority in Christ as a Bishop. After that time, we remained in contact through Facebook and became very good friends.

To cut a long story short, God played 'matchmaker' and he answered not only my prayer for a husband, but also Adrian's prayer for a wife. In 2015 Adrian had asked me to marry him and after saying yes, we considered where we would marry, when we would marry and who would marry us. I of course wanted a big wedding with all my friends and family but as we both were on our third marriage and we both were in our fifties. Adrian said he wanted something low key wanting to marry in a Registry Office for the legalities and then go to another country to marry before God, such as Jerusalem. I wasn't happy and became very moody because I knew our friends, family and church wouldn't be happy not being invited. Adrian however was determined to have a private wedding somewhere nice. The only way forward was for both of us to pray and I just felt God say to me to ask Canon Andrew White to marry us. Adrian felt that God wanted us to get married in Jerusalem after signing forms at the Registry Office in Dorchester.

We had our plans but so did God and He never does anything by halves when you are his child as he most certainly isn't a dull or boring Father. He takes you on a journey that for many, they would simply never believe. I knew that it wouldn't be the 'run of the mill' wedding. God showed me a DVD called 'Exodus' about Moses and the plight of the Israelite's and their Exodus from Egypt to Canaan, the 'Promised Land'. This story is recalled in the book of Exodus, Chronicles and Deuteronomy and through this, God showed us His plans to marry in Jerusalem at the time of Passover. First of all, I asked Andrew if he would marry us in Jerusalem, which he agreed to and after a step of faith, Adrian got a gift of money for our wedding but it wasn't quite enough. We therefore prayed to God that if he wanted us to go to Jerusalem, He had to provide enough money for us to book a flight and hotel. A few weeks later, we were given yet another gift for our wedding which meant we could now take care of the legalities at Dorchester Registry Office. We had asked my fiend Anne and my Pastor Pastor Sanjay Sanil, to be our witnesses at the Registry Officer service and asked Sanjay to pray for us throughout the celebration, ending with a meal at Weatherspoon's pub.

Once this part of the wedding process was over, we had to arrange flights and accommodation in Jerusalem. Hotels however were very expensive during Passover, as were flights. At the same time, Andrew was struggling with our dates as he wanted to celebrate his own Wedding Anniversary with Caroline, his wife. Then on top of that, he needed to have stem cell treatment in Baghdad as his MS was progressively getting worse. but he was adamant that he wanted to marry us. All we could do was pray and that's what we did, we prayed and prayed until God came up with a solution. It was a balancing act between Andrew being available, being able to afford the trip and Adrian having time off from work. However, I prayed for keys to open the doors for this wedding and the next thing we knew, I found myself ringing up my good old friend Dougie March, an International Street Evangelist from Byker, Newcastle upon Tyne.

Dougie told me how he had just come back from Israel with Monarch Airlines, who were offering cheap flights to Tel-Aviv. He also mentioned that the Jaffa Hostel near the Jaffa Gate, had very cheap, rates, about twelve pounds a night. When Adrian came home from work, I told him Dougie's news and before I knew it, he had booked the flights with Monarch and 10 nights in Jaffa Hostel. All we had to do now was wait to see when Andrew was free around 21st–24th April, which was right in the middle of Passover. Andrew also had some good news that he would be able to marry us in Christchurch guest house garden, on Passover itself, why we had been invited by Christine Darg's banquet of 'The Seder Marriage of the Lamb' in the evening. As I said, God is the God of the impossible, and the miraculous, especially when you 'Don't care but take risks'.

Our next challenge was that we wanted to give a gift offering to Andrew to support for his school for the Iraqi refugee children in the Lebanon but we had no spare money. I was unemployed and Adrian's money was already spoken for, so my prayer was, "Lord, if you want us to be married in Jerusalem, provide a gift offering for Andrew, you can't shame us, you cannot." A few days later, as I prayed in Adrian's car waiting for him to leave work, God gave me a scripture.

ACTS 5 verses 1-11 Ananias and Sapphira.

1. *Now a man named Ananias, together with his wife, Sapphira, also sold a piece of property.*
2. *With his wife's full knowledge, he kept back part of the money for himself but brought the rest and put it at the apostles' feet.*
3. *Then Peter said, "Ananias, how is it that Satan has so filled your heart that you have lied to the Holy Spirit and have kept for yourself some of the money you received for the land?*
4. *Didn't it belong to you before it was sold? And after it was sold, wasn't the money at your disposal? What made you think of doing such a thing? You have not lied just to human beings but to God."*
5. *When Ananias heard this, he fell down and died. And great fear seized all who heard what had happened.*
6. *Then some young men came forward, wrapped up his body and carried him out and buried him.*
7. *About three hours later, his wife came in, not knowing what had happened.*
8. *Peter asked her, "Tell me, is this the price you and Ananias got for the land?"*
9. *"Yes," she said, "that is the price."*
10. *Peter said to her, "How could you conspire to test the Spirit of the Lord? Listen! The feet of the men who buried your husband are at the door and they will carry you out also."*
11. *At that moment, she fell down at his feet and died. Then the young men came in and finding her dead, carried her out and buried her beside her husband.*

12. Great fear seized the whole church and all who heard about these events.

I felt the Lord speaking to me through this passage that when He had provided the gift offering and we couldn't spend it on anything else, other than the gift offering for Andrew, else there would be serious consequences. After acknowledging God's request, He sent a gift and although it wasn't enough, once Adrian had added some money as did I, the amount seemed acceptable to give to Andrew and all we could do was leave it with the Lord.

Once we settled down, we realised that it was a miracle of God, as we were to have our wedding on the same day as Passover in Jerusalem. Not only that plus we had been invited to the 'Seder marriage of the lamb' with Christine Darg, celebrating the end of the Israelite's exile in Egypt and the plagues that God sent to Pharaoh. Yet again it clearly shows us that God's plans are always the best plans which one couldn't make it up even if you tried. It was green to go, as we really were going to Jerusalem to get married and on a mission; we know that for certain.

The Saturday before our wedding and the beginning of Passover we travelled on a National Express Coach to London Victoria and then on to Luton Airport. Here we slept for a while on the floor as we'd arrived in the early hours of Sunday morning before our flight to Tel Aviv. It was so wonderful to think that God had provided flights and a hostel at such a good price, all thanks to Dougie March. What made the arrangements so miraculous was the fact that it was Passover, normally an expensive time of the year and exceptionally busy as the Jewish people travelled in their droves to Jerusalem, to celebrate this important festival.

Embarrassingly, we didn't realise this until we were sat on the plane eating pork, chicken and bacon sandwiches whilst Jewish men fasted. They were wearing half a coat with the arm tied around their back were wrapping leather around their arm whilst reading Scripture out of two little boxes. Monarch was a disappointment really with no free food and drink and no entertainment on the TV. However, we were able to go to Jerusalem so we thanked God for his provision. We were really happy as we landed in Tel Aviv and it was so much hotter than it was the last time I went to Jerusalem in 2012.

Garden Tomb

Old Jerusalem

Chapter 9

The Seder Marriage of the Lamb

Hanna, Adrian, Elaine, Andrew and Lydia

We sighed a sigh of relief as we got through the security and customs and we were sitting on the shuttle to Jerusalem. It was useful knowing where we were going and where to get off because you could relax and take in the view rather than worrying if we were there yet? Towards the end of the journey, we got talking to an elderly and godly lady called Grace, from New Zealand. She was a very kind lady, we noticed as a young American busker hadn't got enough money to get to where he was going and so she, Grace, gave him enough money to pay the bus driver, of which he was most grateful.

As we got off the mini bus by the Jaffa Gate, Grace also gave a few shekels to a boy who wanted to carry her case in return for money. I wouldn't have done that myself because you don't know what the boy would do with the case but she had a big heart and at the same time couldn't carry it up the steps. Speaking to her a little later by the Jaffa Gate, about her plans, Grace told us she was going to attend to the banquet of the 'Seder Marriage of the Lamb Conference', ran by Christine Darg. It was the same conference that we were invited to and so it wasn't by accident that we met; in fact, she was delighted to hear about our wedding and so it wasn't by chance that we had met.

It was so wonderful to be back in Ha Shem's (God's) compound. What made it even more special was the fact that we were staying inside the walls of 'Old Jerusalem,' next to Christchurch guest house. Our room had the most spectacular view of the Old City overlooking the roof tops of houses, churches, the Dome of the Holy Sepulchre and the Mount of Olives. You could see all the satellite dishes on the roof tops and in the back ground was miles of domes and mosques, some with gold domes and some with green lights. The room was very dusty, and the shower unit was of Middle Eastern standard, although the bed was fairly comfortable which was all that really mattered, because we had such a spectacular view of the Old City to wake up to every morning. It's mind blowing to wake up at 5:30 am and know you are in Jerusalem with views of all the places you wanted to visit and only dreamed about. We both felt like we were home, feeling safe, and I felt close to our Ha Shem, Father God.

The only challenge we both had was the sound of church bells ringing every few hours. CLANG! CLANG! CLANG! CLANG! In England, bell ringers are trained to make a wonderful sound, but here it was loud and very dull, not like our tuneful bells, when of course in tune. We also had men calling out in their Arabic language prayers from the Koran in the Mosques. At one point, they sounded like wasps. However, as time went by, both the clanging bells and the wailing men in the Mosques, seemed to be in competition with each other which to be honest, was very hard on the ears.

Apart from the view, the good thing was the room was made of stone and so when it was very hot outside it was cool inside, plus we were relatively safe as the outer door was locked and you had to pass the reception to be able to get to the rooms. A friendly Palestinian family ran the hostel who were very pleasant not forceful like some places I had been to wanting you to pay for this trip in advance. They just seemed to want to make a living and were pleasant whilst leaving you to get on with your holiday.

The night we arrived, we had 'Fish 'n' Chips', in a restaurant run by the Christian Orthodox Church, not far from our Hostel. It was wonderful food and most welcome after all that travelling, as was the 'Maccabee Beer', which was a little expensive. This was because the Jewish quarter's wouldn't sell beer at Passover, as it wasn't kosher,) and this meant we could only afford one glass each.

We woke up the next day very early and as we looked out of the window, we saw the Glory of God shining over Jerusalem and even the clanging bells were welcome. It uplifted the soul, to know you were in the City of the Great King, the Daughter of Zion, a joy to all the Earth.

By 8 am, we had a pot of porridge, pot noodle and hummus with 'cheese and tomato'. On another occasion, we had oranges, yogurt with nuts, and sometimes we had sausage meat made out of chicken, as they wouldn't eat pork sausage, as pork isn't Kosher. Sometimes we had instant potato mash mixed with hot water. As the kettle was downstairs and the Wi-Fi, it only made sense to use this time to check Facebook, and emails discovering that a No 12 bus in Jerusalem had been blown up by terrorists, we decided to let people know that we were safe, else they'd only worry. After breakfast, we went for a walk to visit the Garden Tomb, walking through the Market in the Old City on the way. As we left the Hostel, the first person we bumped into was Michael, a Jewish guy from UK. Michael told us that he was a resident in the hostel for six months at a time. He was a very genuine person with a very soft heart, plus a man of God. Michael mentioned we should visit the Western Wall very early in the morning, as the Aaronite's, would be coming to make a special blessing over the people of Jerusalem for Passover.

Christchurch guest house and Christian retreat centre, was the first point of call where we were going to be married in the garden and it was lovely to feel the presence of God as we sat in their beautiful Church listening to a man playing Christian worship music on the piano. He was very good, especially when he played 'Jerusalem' which echo led all round the inner Church . At the same time, we were in one of the beautiful stained-glass windows depicting an Olive Tree with a mysterious message of the the two broken off branches, connected by Hebrew characters and we read:

"Ba rachamim asher ha shemesh alechem yerachamu gam hem ke'at."

Which means: 'By the mercy of God, who makes the sun shine above you, lovingness will be given to you in our days'. King David saw himself as an Olive Tree as it says in Psalms 52:8 But I am like a green Olive Tree in the house of God; I trust in the mercy of God forever and ever.

However is said to be aimed at the Jewish people as they feel abandoned by God with their painful past. Why the Jewish people need Yeshua Messiah, as they are still waiting for their Messiah, but in Yeshua him, they will find hope and salvation.

Christchurch Christian Center, itself has a lot of History as it is the first Protestant Church in whole of the Middle East to be built on the site of Herod's Palace where Jesus /Yeshua was said to have been sent to trial after his arrest. We bumped into Grace again and we chatted for a bit as she wanted to come to our wedding led by Canon Andrew White ,and so we invited her to come along and told her she was more than welcome.

The Garden Tomb, near the Damascus Gate, was the next point of call. As usual once we got to the Garden Tomb, it was a very emotional experience to visit the place where Jesus/ Yeshua, is said to have risen from the grave after three days, after being crucified. It was very hard not to shed a tear at this site, whilst feeling extremely humble to think that Jesus had been crucified as a Sacrificial Lamb, for the redemption of our, my sin. However, God has a great sense of humour, as above Golgotha (place of the skull) is a Muslim graveyard and below is a Muslim bus station, with a mosque next door. Whilst in the beautiful garden, we joined a group from Indonesia who had travelled all the way to Israel to see where their Saviour died and rose again after three days. We took the opportunity to sing together and we also prayed for them that God would bless them and impart His Holy Spirit upon them. The flowers and foliage in the garden were exquisite, a very fitting place that Joseph of Arimathea whose grave it was, was to bury Jesus. Inside the tomb, above the door it reads, "He is not here, for He is risen!"

Nearby the empty tomb was a wine press that they thought was owned and used by tin miner Joseph of Arimathea, who in English folklore is said to have brought his cousin Mary, mother of Jesus, and her mother to Cornwall and Glastonbury, after Jesus was crucified, to escape the hands of the Jewish and Romans Leaders.

As it was Passover only, Kosher food was on the menu apart from in the 'Arab Quarters' so we were really stuck for simple food like bread as it wasn't unleavened and, therefore, we couldn't make sandwiches or make toast. Instead, the only other option was to have falafel in the Damascus Gate or in the Old City market, and although they were nice, they weren't substantial. It was so hot as we walked back to the

Jaffa Gate through the Market inside the Old City which was heaving with people and people pushing carts overflowing with boxes and 'general wares'. It was so steep climbing upwards, towards our hostel walking up and up and up for miles and every time you thought you were getting somewhere you realised that you still hadn't reached the Jaffa Gate.

Andrew, who had been chatting to us on Facebook, told us when he would be arriving and that he planned to take us to the real place where the last supper had taken place, which was down some steps rather than the site where you had to walk up steps near 'David's Tomb'. He had suggested we would get married there, but Andrew had been struggling walking and was having to use a wheelchair and that's why we were going to get married in Christchurch Garden instead.

The following day, we walked to David's Tomb and it was like a small synagogue, as the Tomb had two partitions, one side for the men and the other for the women. As I went in the Tomb area on the women's side, I was told to take off my clergy collar and was also told to take off my cross, but I refused. I simply just didn't want to compromise my faith and I wondered how would they feel if I told them to take off their Kippah, their Jewish hat, if they entered a church? Adrian had tucked his cross away in his pocket and so hadn't been told to remove his cross or collar.

The next port of call was a Roman Catholic Church of Saint Peter in Gallicantu, Jerusalem located on the eastern slope of Mount Zion, just outside the Old Walled City of Jerusalem. The view was awesome especially the view of the Kidron valley and Bethlehem. The church takes its name from the Latin word 'Gallicantu, meaning 'cock crow'. It was a place that depicts Peter's triple denial of Jesus before the cock crowed, Mark 13 v30. It is said that it is here that Caiaphas had his palace which is why they believe this is where Jesus was taken before the Sanhedrin who accused him of being the 'King of the Jews'. Adrian and I began to sing modern hymns and prayed for the Peace of Jerusalem in the first church we went in to, and couldn't help but stare at the ceiling with its beautiful mosaics taken from the New Testament,. The Mosaic's were made from tiny pieces of stone, which were phenomenal. Downstairs was a Chapel built into the rock which was a much simpler Church, without all the iconic pictures and you sensed the peace of the Lord and His presence why people prayed there to find God.

As we walked down another flight of stairs, we came to a series of chambers and caves and it is said that it is here where Jesus was taken to after he was arrested to be imprisoned. It is also rumoured to have been where the disciples were held and flogged with a whip for preaching the Gospel in Jerusalem… You could see metal and leather chains knocked into the wall where they would have been scourged and left for days, unless the Angels came to their rescue. There was one cave where everybody seemed to gather singing 'Amazing Grace' and then we all read Psalm 88 written on a card in many different languages.

Psalm 88

1. *O Lord, God of my salvation; I cry out day and night before you.*
2. *Let my prayer come before you; incline your ear to my cry!*

3. *For my soul is full of troubles, and my life draws near to Sheol.*
4. *I am counted among those who go down to the pit; I am a man who has no strength,*
5. *like one set loose among the dead, like the slain that lie in the grave, like those whom you remember no more, for they are cut off from your hand.*
6. *You have put me in the depths of the pit, in the regions dark and deep.*
7. *Your wrath lies heavy upon me, and you overwhelm me with all your waves. Selah*
8. *You have caused my companions to shun me; you have made me a horror to them. I am shut in so that I cannot escape;*
9. *my eye grows dim through sorrow. Every day, I call upon you, O Lord; I spread out my hands to you.*
10. *Do you work wonders for the dead? Do the departed rise up to praise you? Selah*
11. *Is your steadfast love declared in the grave, or your faithfulness in Destruction?*
12. *Are your wonders known in the darkness, or your righteousness in the land of forgetfulness?*
13. *But I, O Lord, cry to you; in the morning my prayer comes before you.*
14. *O Lord, we do you cast my soul away? Why do you hide your face from me?*
15. *Afflicted and close to death from my youth up, I suffer your terrors; I am helpless.*
16. *Your wrath has swept over me; your dreadful assaults destroy me.*

17. They surround me like a flood all day long; they close in on me together.

18. You have caused my beloved and my friend to shun me; my companions have become darkness.

Outside, there were beautiful flowers with sweet smelling roses, a smell I hadn't smelt for years since I was a child, they were simply gorgeous. We enjoyed looking at the model of Old Jerusalem how it would have looked in Jesus time and also the ruins of Caiaphas Palace where he would have lived. It was so wonderful to see the Bible coming alive in the Father God's compound'

We carried on walking in the heat and passed the Golden Gates where it is said that Jesus will return and enter Jerusalem. A bit further down the hill there was Mary's Tomb in a very poorly lit church, with steep steps leading down to the base of the shrine with endless icons, lamps and chandeliers. It really did smell of smoke and incense why it almost caused you to choke and you could hardly see anything. It was so smokey from incense, that the glass was covered with what looked like soot.

I was horrified to see people kissing Mary's Tomb and putting money into the shrine and I actually believe that Mary would be horrified too, to see this going on as Jesus didn't like graven images. A few years ago, however, I wouldn't have entered the shrine but since studying Mary in the Bible, I found that she was the Arc of the Covenant as she carried Jesus in her womb for nine months, a very important person to Jesus as his mother and helper of his Ministry and Mary was a very key person to the early church. However, over the years, some denominations have almost demonised her which is very wrong. The olive trees in the Garden of Gethsemane, a little further up from her shrine, were very old with thick trunks and it is believed that they were two thousand years old. These trees are very likely to have been around at the time of Jesus/ Yeshua Messiah, when He came to pray at the garden before his arrest.

The church next to the gardens was very iconic with lots of beautiful pictures and many, many people gathered in the church taking photos and contemplating about God. For me it was very suffocating being extremely hot and with all those people milling around and so we left and turned back to the Lyon's Gate.

After walking and walking and more walking, getting cross with people who stood staring into space, as their tour guide gave instructions and information about different stations of the cross, blocking the pathways, we decided to go back to the garden tomb and rest. This we did but it was simply too hot and after falafel at the Damascus Gate, we headed back to the hostel on a Tram.

We got off in the New modern City of Jerusalem, with shops, bars, Cofix, 6 Shekel food shops, linen shops and Bible shops and then walked down to the Old City via the Old City Walls, heading back to the Jaffa Gate.' Despite our little annoyance, one good thing about the day was that we had achieved what we had set out to do. Now the Bible was coming alive and all the things God had been showing us were beginning to make sense and take shape.

After prayers on the roof, we heard that Andrew was now on his way to Jerusalem and we began to get excited about our wedding day. Before we went to bed, we decided not to go on a trek around the Old City but we would go on the tram and visit the King of Kings Prayer Tower, where they have 24/7 prayer going on night and day. They prayed for the Peace of Jerusalem, and also for the Jews to come to faith with Yeshua and for all the nations of the World.

I wanted to show Adrian where I had spent three nights in prayer the last time that I had visited Jerusalem. I so enjoyed having the privilege of praying for 'Peace in Jerusalem' and for other Nations.

It was such a contrast going on the tram in the New Modern City of Jerusalem. A different vibrant new city that was being built up more and more. After going through security in the tower block where the prayer centre was, we went up the lift to the fourteenth floor and walked around the Prayer Tower looking out the windows and praying all around Jerusalem from different angles and sides.

Adrian was in awe and wonder as we prayed for the 'Peace of Jerusalem', and my prayer was that today God would show all the peoples of all the Nations how much He loves them, Jew, Gentile, Arab and Greek, Rich or Poor Slave or Free. As we went in to the worship room listening first of all to the Song of songs session, I was quiet and didn't speak I just began to read the Bible.

As I did this, God gave me a vision of Jesus on the cross but only his head with a crown of thorns, with his head hung down as tears were flowing from his eyes, like a fountain. I could almost hear Jesus/Yeshua crying for the lost, those heading for hell and for His Bride (the church) who are fast asleep, in a spiritual coma, not getting ready for the Groom to come back in all His Glory. The Gospel wasn't being preached or talks about Hell and Heaven and the verse came to mind, "Without knowledge my people will perish. If my people who are called by my Name, would repent and humble themselves and pray and seek my face, and turn from their wicked ways, then I will hear from heaven, forgive and heal their land."

I also read in the Bible about how the Jews in the Old Testament were marrying women from places with other gods and who worshipped idolatry. Also about how people were practising witchcraft, idolatry and immorality etc. This was then confirmed the next day by Michael who told me that many young Jewish people are marrying Muslims, and converting to that religion because they are listening to propaganda that's been spread in Jerusalem. Also, I heard Muslim men were marrying Jewish girls and then making them become Muslims after being very brutal to them.

The next session, as we were sitting in the room on our own, Adrian and I were reading scripture from the Bible and we prayed for the land whilst dancing before the Lord and we both felt the Presence of God strongly. Later on, we were joined by a few others and found ourselves praying for Pastors who had Churches both in Israel and Jerusalem. Later on, we were joined by Daniel an Evangelist from Korea so we both prayed for Daniel which blessed him greatly.

That evening, we were so happy to see Andrew who had just arrived from the UK and was sitting on his bed with his laptop on his knee, surrounded by cases, papers and presents, especially for Hanna's children. I was so glad to see him after such a long time over five years since I visited Baghdad. Adrian was delighted to meet the man I never stop talking about. We chatted about how Adrian and I had met and about our wedding in Christchurch guest house, and retreat centre Garden. Andrew then told us about the story of his watch which he bought his son Jacob one Christmas.

Jacob wouldn't wear his watch because it was too old-fashioned for him, only being a young man and so when his father asked if he could borrow it until he could buy another one, Jacob said he couldn't borrow it but he should rather buy it from him for $200. One may think that wasn't very nice of Jacob but actually it shows Jacob was an entrepreneur and a sign of being a great businessman and so we all laughed. Andrew also told us how he had bought Caroline a huge silver model of Jerusalem for their anniversary, which they had just celebrated before he came to Jerusalem to marry us.

Later on, his assistant Peter came armed with presents that Andrew had sent him shopping for, including a beautiful Hebrew Certificate for our wedding day, and a silver communion cup with Old Jerusalem inscribed around it, as well as a matching saucer. Wow, we felt so humbled, honoured and so embarrassed because Andrew had really lavished such generosity on us, yet we had little to give him in return.

Andrew was falling asleep and so went back to the hostel and returned to Christchurch guest house, an hour or so later where we met Hanna and his children. Hanna was Andrew's Jerusalem Factotum, and he had worked with Andrew and known him for many, many, many years. This is why Andrew had bought laptops for all of Hanna's children for a joint Easter and Passover gift which they all loved.

Andrew is a very generous man indeed as the following evening, he took us to dinner at The King David Hotel, a key place for political and historical deals to have been made and also where the rich and famous stayed, they even had a hall of fame where famous people had signed their signature on special tiles on the floor like Obama and other Presidents, or used their thumbprint like Stephen Hawking. It was such a beautiful place and such an honour to be taken there for dinner as the food was delightful. We were joined by a beautiful girl called Lydia, from Armenia, who worked as a volunteer at Christchurch guest house, she was a really lovely girl and one of Andrew's adopted children.

Whilst eating our food, Andrew got talking to a Jewish Banker from Wall Street USA whose wife was a Rabbi. It's truly amazing how God takes us to places we never thought we would go to and do things we never thought we would do and meet people we never thought in a million years we would meet! We had fish and chips, salad and a glass of wine whilst Andrew and Lydia had juice followed by Ice cream and coffee and Adrian had tea. The tea bags were beautiful as they came in a little silky bag inside a beautifully decorated box which was very swish. Hanna joined us before we left and then we went back to Christchurch guest house in the black vehicle that look bullet proof.

As we went back to the Jaffa Gate, Andrew explained how they were involved with the hostage situation in Bethlehem some years ago where people were held captive by terrorists. As they drove towards Bethlehem, an Israeli tank hit them and so Hanna got out of their car and asked if the tank was insured! After dropping Lydia off, we went back to the hostel and planned for the wedding the next day.

The following day, we both had little money left but as Andrew had done so much for us, we agreed we had to buy him a personal gift to thank him for all he done because we wanted to show him, we loved him dearly. With little time before the wedding, we walked into the market to see what we could find but the market was like a rabbit warren in the old part of the city and we struggled to find anything suitable that he may like? As time going by fast, we found nothing that was suitable and so we prayed and we saw a silver pen holder with a Jerusalem ball on top of the star of David. Too much choice, far too much choice, we thought but we went with the pen rest as I knew Andrew collects expensive pens.

Time was still on our side and so we went to the Holy Sepulchre and as it was early morning there were very few tourists, only the archaeologists preparing a mosaic. We saw where Jesus was placed in a tomb but it didn't have the same feeling as the Garden Tomb at all, even though the Holy Sepulchre was empty of people. I did pray and asked the Lord "which tomb did you rise from, from the dead, the Garden Tomb or here?" Then the presence of the Lord came over me and said, "I am everywhere." He reassured me that the main thing was that He was risen and not in the tomb.

Back at the hostel, we changed into our wedding clothes. I wore my long flowing skirt, white top and a cream jacket with a white scarf around my head. I didn't look too bad but I didn't want to wear a long white wedding dress with a veil, as this would be my third marriage and for a 54-year-old woman, in my train of thought, was stupid. Adrian wore black trousers, black shirt and a white waist coat that I had bought him a few years ago, which looking back was prophetic. I must say Adrian did look very smart and also Jewish.

By 11 am, we had walked over to the church and found Andrew sitting with a couple whose marriage he had blessed six months earlier. Daniel originally from the Ararat area of Armenia and his wife, Esti, from USA would be our witnesses for our wedding. Grace was there too, although she thought the wedding would be 5 pm, not 11 am but God knew she had promised to come and so it was the hand of God that had brought her to Christchurch guest house as she was staying in a different hotel.

Andrew announced that all Jewish weddings were performed outside, why we were to have the ceremony under a 'hooper' and arch made from a vine but this case a rose tree How romantic! Andrew gave us a choice of which robe we wanted him to wear, either a white one or red, and we chose the red one., as its the sign of royal and special occasions. There we were in the garden at Christchurch guest house and Christian retreat centre, in Jerusalem, being married by Canon Andrew White, the Vicar of Baghdad. Our witnesses were Esti and Daniel, Grace and Hanna and Lydia, whom we met at King David's Hotel the night before. Andrew read out various scriptures and instructions in Hebrew and somehow as Andrew was talking the juice in the cup, it fell over onto the lovely certificate. "Oh, NO!" we all thought, but Andrew very quickly wiped off the juice and there was no damage to it at all. Lydia said that our wedding was more enjoyable than a normal wedding as it was more personal and natural. Adrian and I felt the same as it was unique, especially as Andrew used his same pen with same green ink to sign our Hebrew Marriage certificate, as Mr Raouf, Minister of Justice for Iraq, signed the death warrant with of Saddam Hussein which he borrowed from Andrew. You couldn't make it up.

Elaine and Adrian about to get married

Our Hebrew Marriage Certificate, signed with Andrew's green ink pen, the same pen that Mr Raouf used to sign Saddam's death warrant!

God told me to throw the flowers I held on my wedding day to Lydia, as she was looking for a husband and she caught them, wow! Andrew then blessed Daniel and Esti's marriage and I prayed for Esti because she had mentioned that her sisters were barren and she wanted children, so I prayed for God to cut her off from a barren womb and God would make her fruitful. (Up to now, she has three sons and a daughter that's a real answer to prayer).

Once we had had cake and tea for our wedding refreshments, we went back to our hostel for a rest before the Seder Marriage Banquet of the Lamb, hosted by Christine Darg and her ministry. We all met up at Christchurch guest house and Daniel plus Andrew's aide, Adrian and Esti helped push Andrew across the cobble streets all uphill with bags. Andrew was also helped with his books that were for sale in boxes. I think they really enjoyed helping Andrew, it helped us bond as a group.

Thankfully the restaurant where the banquet was being held, was in the Armenian Quarter. The room was beautiful and all set out in a super like a really special feast and it had place mats, cutlery set out properly and I felt very privileged to meet Christine Darg the lady who hosts Jerusalem TV. I took to Christine Darg Immediately, as you could see she was a woman who loved Yeshua and had a big heart for Jewish people. Christine she really was just such a nice person. Adrian and I sat at the head table with Andrew and Christine and a few others sat next to us and so we felt really welcomed and honoured as the 'Bride and Groom' They also honoured Esti and Daniel because Andrew had recently married them too. After Christine gave a short talk, we began to take part in the Seder Meal and each item on the Seder plate represented something that signified the Hebrew people being freed from slavery in Egypt.

Pharaoh refused free God's people even after he and the Egyptians had suffered from several plagues, and it wasn't until the 'Angel of Death' came upon the firstborn of the Egyptian people, including Pharaoh. It was only when his own firstborn son died that he set God's People free to leave for the promised land. The Jews, however, were protected from the 'Angel of Death' because that they had painted Lamb's blood on their door posts as protection. This is where I realised why God had been telling us to watch the new Moses film. Now the Seder Meal now made sense, bringing the Word of God alive. Firstly, the Haggadah is read which contains the narrative of the Israelite Exodus from Egypt with a special blessing and rituals and commentaries from the Talmud and some special Passover songs.

Seder Meal (Passover meal) and Customs

1. *Telling the story of Passover, discussing the story of Passover.*
2. *Drinking four cups of wine to celebrate how God redeemed and rescued the Israelite's then led them from slavery out of Egypt and restored them by taking them to the promised land.*
3. *Matzo bread has no leaven in it as yeast is forbidden at the time of Passover.*
4. *Maror, bitter herbs are eaten like horseradish to recall bitterness of slavery.*
5. *Charoset, a brown sweet paste made of nuts, apples, wine and cinnamon which is put on put on the Matzo to remind us of the mortar the Israelite slaves made for the bricks during their slavery.*

6. *Spring onion represent the task masters whipping the slaves to work harder.*
7. *Salt water represents the tears that were shed during the time of slavery.*
8. *Beitzah a roasted egg is eaten as it shows the hotter you make it for the Israelite's the tougher they become as a people.*
9. *Karpas which means green vegetable which they rarely are because vegetables were so scarce in Egypt.*
10. *A lamb shank is roasted and eaten as a mark of respect to the temple sacrifices to God.*

During the Seder Meal, I spilled water and knocked wine all over the table cloth, thankfully it didn't cause too much of a scene, whilst a large blue bottle fly, put me off from eating an egg as it sat right on top it. Christine Darg had placed a gift for us on the table and she gave me a wonderful necklace and earrings resembling the Arc of the Covenant which were very prophetic and also very beautiful.

During a talk by a member of Christine's ministry, it was very interesting to hear that the Catholic Church moved their Easter from the same time as Jewish Passover to the times of the pagans. This is why Christians celebrate Easter and the Passover is celebrated by the Jews, Messianic Jews and some Christians like Christine Darg and those who are a part of her ministry. The Orthodox Jews and others celebrate passover on another date and I began to understand why God was clearly teaching me all about this before I came to Jerusalem.

Adrian and Daniel both prayed and then I read Psalm 24, "Uplifted are you, gates; be lifted up, you, ancient doors in Jerusalem, and let the King of Glory come in. Who is this

King of Glory? The Lord Almighty, he is the King of Glory." Later on, God told me that he gave me this Psalms to read as he was speaking to me about the Golden Gate, closed hundreds of years previously by a Muslim ruler. The Muslim ruler wanted to stop Yeshua / Jesus from coming through it when he returns. In the Bible it says Yeshua will come back on the mount of Olives then and He will enter through the Golden Gate regardless to Jerusalem

By the time the event had finished, my brain had scrambled because with the combination of just getting married and the wonderful Wedding Banquet with Andrew and his good friend Christine Darg and brain damage from Cerebral Malaria I was struggling to cope, why I am sure Andrew must have felt the same having MS. Having an illness isn't easy if you are always busy, on the go and sometimes you get to the point where it all gets too much. Before the wonderful banquet a lady gave Esti some beautiful flowers and I was given a bouquet by another lady but sadly due to the heat of the day they looked worse for wear. I must admit I was a bit miffed that Esti had been given the nice ones as we were the ones who had got married. When we got back to Christchurch guest house, Andrew who by now was sat on a chair in reception took one look at the bouquet and told me they looked terrible and before I knew it, he took them and put them in the bin. Andrew did make us laugh although it was a kind thought of the lady it was just the heat of the day had wilted them, bless Esti though as she had given me the flowers that were given to her.

The following day, we went back to the garden tomb and then on to a Prayer Centre near not far from St George's Cathedral on Nablus Road. It was a big beautiful house run by the Southern Baptist Church of America, which the last time I visited it was being served by Bob and his wife. This year there were two other couples serving in the Prayer centre who were equally as friendly. The house was surrounded by a beautiful garden and inside the Prayer Centre's chapel was a piano, and on the wall was a Mural painted by a Messianic Jewish lady, and it was of the tree with the leaves, of the healing of the Nation and all fruits that grow in Israel entwined with a vine, Revelation 22: Verse 2.

Upstairs there was a prayer room where you could draw prophetically, put names of loved ones needing prayer on stones, write prayers on paper and put them in a box to be read out and maps of the world on the walls where you could pray for different nations. There were lots of Bibles and books in lovely wooden book shelves, plus a place to meditate on God and I drew the vision I had in the Prayer Tower, of the picture of the face of Jesus with the crown of thorns crying for the lost. Before we left to go to St George's Cathedral, we went downstairs and had a time of prayer with one of the couples who worked in the Southern Baptist prayer house, to thank them for what they were doing and for praying for the Peace of Jerusalem.

What was very special about going to St George's was that fact that it was St George's day. It was a lovely Anglican Cathedral and inside a lady was playing an organ and as we walked down the aisle, it was like 'The Wedding March' that I had longed for us to take part in and it was if God had orchestrated it. Like the Southern Baptist, Prayer Centre, the cathedral had beautiful flowers in their garden including sweet smelling roses, palms trees and wall flowers which were outstandingly beautiful.

By now we were very hungry and so we bought a falafel from a street vendor and sat down on the steps of circular arena at the Damascus Gate. As I looked up, I saw a man wearing a scarf aiming a gun right at me and I thought," *Oh my goodness, it's a terrorist."* Thankfully it was an Israeli soldier guarding the Damascus Gate. Nevertheless, Adrian and I moved out of the line of fire as we both felt very uncomfortable. When we arrived at the Hostel, Michael came and told us that the Aaronite Cohanim, were coming to The Western Wall very early the following morning to bless the Jewish people and so we decided we would go. Aaronite's are Jewish Priests whose job it was to protect and serve in the Temple and who come from the Tribe of Levi through the line of Aaron who was Moses' brother. This is why the Aaronite's are seen as being anointed. This was the first time in a long period of time that they went to the The Western Wall during Passover. They went to bless the people remembering Moses and Aaron leading the Hebrews out of Egypt and in to the promised land.

We got up very early but unfortunately Michael wasn't there as he must have gone to the Western Wall at the crack of dawn. It was incredibly hot and the small streets in the Old City where the markets are were crammed with Jewish people rushing to get to the Western Wall, as quickly as possible see the Cohanim, why the Israeli soldiers where out in force worried that there would be a terrorist attack. We managed to get to the Western Wall, after queuing behind a number of Jewish people at the security barriers waiting to be searched and then push our way through a sea of people to the railings where you could just about see the Aaronite's.

It was very difficult to keep a track on what they were doing with hundreds of Jewish men and women standing in front of us in their sections This is why I was thankful that Adrian had taken his binoculars which greatly improved our vision of the Aaronite Priests. However, it was still a privileged to be there and hear the scripture and blessing over the people.

Adrian and I were standing right next to the Rabbi who was reading out portions of scripture from Numbers 6; "This is the law of the Nazirite who vows offerings to the Lord in accordance with their dedication, in addition to whatever else they can afford."

"They must fulfil the vows they have made, according to the law of the Nazirite." (A Nazirite is one who voluntarily took a vow described in Number 6: Verse 1–21)

The Priestly Blessing Numbers 6: Verse 22-27

22. The Lord said to Moses,
23. Tell Aaron and his sons, "This is how you are to bless the Israelites." Say to them:
24. "The Lord bless you and keep you;
25. The Lord makes his face shine on you and be gracious to you;
26. The Lord turns his face towards you and gives you peace.
27. So they will put my name on the Israelite, and I will bless them."

Even if we didn't understand Hebrew or Aramaic, it was wonderful just to be there and wonderful to be a part of the blessing.

There was a tour which took you under the Western Wall, to visit the original city wall and the streets that were around at the time of Jesus and so we booked a tour at 11:40 which gave us time to rest as we were very tired after such an early start. I had to keep sitting down as in old Jerusalem you had to walk everywhere and it was all up and down steep pathways. As I rested, I saw a blind Muslim man who I felt led to pray for, however, I didn't know what to do as we couldn't speak the same language, and Muslims had strict rules and regulations about what women can and can't do. Instead I prayed quietly for him. I felt led to pray for people on a number of occasions but although I had the desire to pray for the person, I didn't because I feared their reaction which I have regretted ever since.

There were long queues of people waiting to go on the tour under the Western Wall, why Adrian and I got lost trying to find our English-speaking tour guide and ended up where only women were allowed to pray at foundations of the Western Wall. In fact it was closer to the original Western Wall than where the men danced, prayed and sang in an underground Synagogue. It was fascinating to watch the men dancing and singing as they were very joyous in their praises, in fact, it looked a bit like our charismatic worship.

However, after backtracking to where we had begun the tour, we managed to find our tour guide almost finishing his explanation as to how skilled men had to carve the top of Mount Moriah by hand to make a flat surface, so that they could build the Temple on the Temple Mount. The tour guide also explained that at the time when the Dome of the Rock was built on the Temple Mount, Mohammed wasn't even in existence and so it hadn't been built towards Mecca, plus the words written inside the Dome of the Rock, didn't mention anything about Mohammed. According to the tour guide, it wasn't a Muslim temple, as the Muslim faith started after the temple was built. However, how true this information is, I really don't know, whether it was his opinion or was it a fact? We also heard that the original Temple was built in David's city not on the Temple Mount.

The further down we managed to walk thorough narrow tunnels and along the old walk ways, we noticed that the stones of the Old Wall were made from huge pieces of rock and we wondered how they managed to move huge pieces of rock from Zedekiah's cave to the Temple wall. I had watched a YouTube documentary where it has stated that in those days, there were giants called 'Nephilim' who had become slaves and used to move the stones. It may seem far-fetched but it would make sense and there have been skeletons of giants found in Israel. And all over the world. Amazingly as we looked into the rocks, Adrian and I were drawn to stone that had what seemed like the face of Jesus cut into the rock, similar to one that we noticed in Zedekiah cave. Unfortunately, the makeshift electric lighting had cut out and because it was pitch black due to health and safety reason, we had to turn around and go back. However, the tour guide incorporated visiting lots of ancient underground water cisterns to make up for the short tour. He said that because it only rained six months of the year, they made underground water cisterns to save water for times of drought.

Once we had finished the tour and visited the Garden Tomb where we prayed and had something to eat by the Damascus Gate and then travelled back to the hostel on the Jerusalem electric tram as we couldn't face any more walking.

After resting for a while, we went to Christchurch guest house and Christian retreat centre, to a healing service with Christine Darg but sadly had to leave as I became very ill with high fever from recurring malaria. Amazingly as I cried out to God to be healed, He told me to go to the Golden Gate by the Temple Mount the following day with a Bible and pray in the Holy Spirit for the doors to open that the King of Glory shall come in.

The following day, both feeling exhausted and as I am not a great lover of walking, I was more than happy to stay in the hostel and have a rest but Adrian told me we had to go to the Golden Gate as this is what God had commanded me to do. I really just wanted a rest as after all it was our honeymoon, but if God says to do something, you have to do it. This is what we did and so off we went, this time we went via the Jewish Quarters past the Western Wall through the Dung Gate.

Looking at the map, we had to turn left and go through a Muslim burial ground which ran alongside the outer wall by the Temple Mount and then to the Golden Gate, known also as the Gate of Mercy. In Hebrew it means 'Sha'ar Ha Rachamim'. It is the only Eastern Gate of the Temple Mount, and one of only two that are used to offer access in the city. the Golden Gate has had its doors closed since medieval times because the Muslim leader at the time, didn't want Jesus to go through the gate when 'He' returns but who can stop the Lord Almighty. As we came to the Muslim graveyard, which looked very derelict, we walked very slowly along the path by the graves stones and I felt really vulnerable, wondering if we would get shot by terrorists or Palestinian sympathisers?

You may think I was being very hysterical and over-reacting but it has happened to me before when I had visited

Jerusalem in 2010. I kept saying to Adrian we can't go to the Golden Gate, let's pray here and go back but Adrian was adamant that we did what God had instructed us to do. God did ease my mind because another couple passed us, walking the opposite way, who commented that it was safe to walk there and nothing had happened to them. When we saw the Golden Gate, we prayed over the land and over all the Wall's Gates and read Psalm 24.

I tore Psalm 24 out of the Gideon's Bible so that Adrian could put it in a rock near the Golden Gate, as we prayed that God would smash those walls down and let Jesus in, the King of Glory, it was mind blowing to see how God was using us, even though we don't quite understand why or what would come out of the prayers. It was all done in Faith. Once back in the hostel, we went on the rooftop and sat and prayed again for the Golden Gate to be opened and let the King of Glory in. Amen.

Psalm 24
A Psalm of David.

1. *The Earth is the Lord's and the fullness thereof; the world, and they that dwell therein.*
2. *For he hath founded it upon the seas and established it upon the floods.*
3. *Who shall ascend into the hill of the Lord? or who shall stand in his holy place?*
4. *He that hath clean hands and a pure heart; who hath not lifted up his soul unto vanity, nor sworn deceitfully.*
5. *He shall receive the blessing from the Lord and righteousness from the God of his salvation.*

6. *This is the generation of them that seek him, that seek thy face, O Jacob. Selah.*
7. *Lift up your heads, O ye gates; and be ye lift up, ye everlasting doors; and the King of glory shall come in.*
8. *Who is this King of glory? The Lord strong and mighty, the Lord mighty in battle.*
9. *Lift up your heads, O ye gates; even lift them up, ye everlasting doors; and the King of glory shall come in.*
10. *Who is this King of glory? The Lord of hosts, he is the King of glory. Selah.*

The following day, we got up at the crack of dawn and walked to the Mount of Olives at 5:30 am when it was very cool and misty. At this time, there was nobody about only an odd Jewish man going to the Western Wall and soldiers on patrol, although there was a lady in a wheelchair and yet again, I felt led to pray for her but didn't because of lack of faith and confidence. Instead I prayed a prayer in my head. I had also wanted to preach the Gospel in Jerusalem but with prayer, I had lack of faith and missed out on God opportunities of which I regret greatly.

We seemed to have been walking for ages and the streets look so different and much bigger when there was nobody about. We walked down by the Lyon Gate after getting lost and then up a steep narrow road to the Garden of Gethsemane and a little further we began our ascent to the Mount of Olives. I don't like walking and it was hard going walking up a steep slope so much so I had to ask God to help me. "We can do all things through Christ Jesus," I kept repeating over and over and over again and He did, praise Yeshua Messiah. I kept stopping praying for Jerusalem and stopping and praying for peace and for Poole in England and all the Nations and stopping and praying for Chungni Suna Migori Kenya, and people like Challis etc. As we walked around the corner, the view was awesome of Old Jerusalem and of the Golden Temple and the Golden Gate, so we prayed Psalm 24 again and again.

Once you got to the top, you could see the Kidron Valley and the Palestinian areas and the way towards Bethlehem. Wow it was awesome! I couldn't help but sing Luo songs and modern worship songs. It was so spiritual knowing this is where Yeshua will return to, especially as it was just Adrian and myself on the Temple Mount plus a guard sitting in a security box. There were no people, no camels, no pick pockets just me Adrian and God and the security guard.

The climb was worth every minute of our struggles but I did wonder where Jesus would stand when He returns as everywhere is taken up with, Jewish graves, very old olive trees and Camels, parking spaces for coaches, plus millions of people visiting the area every day. Going down the hill was quicker than walking up the twisty narrow road, why we went back a different way. On the way back we came across Haggai's grave and also that of two minor prophets but at 7 a.m. early in the morning we found the site to be closed.

We tried to make the journey even shorter and walked through the Jewish graveyard and then through the Kidron Valley where Jesus would have walked. It was here that we came across a Bedouin and his tent with a couple of men feeding a camel. They seemed like nice guys so we waved and greeted them with a good morning, and thy waved and smiled back, but we didn't stop, we carried on walking before it got very very hot.

Even though we had to climb up many steps to get back to the Dung Gate, I didn't mind as by now after over a week of climbing up and down hills and steps in Jerusalem, I was getting very fit. We were walking everywhere and by this point, we were both hungry and fed up with walking and decided to go back to the Garden Tomb just one more time. It was our last chance to say prayers at the site of the tomb where Yeshua rose from the dead and also buy gifts.

I am glad we did go back as God gave me a wonderful opportunity to pray for a man called Ed. As we were praying at the tomb, I kept hearing God telling me to pray for the man sitting on the bench opposite who was with his wife. Once I had got myself together and plucked up courage I went over and chatted to Ed. He told me he had MS, so we both prayed for him and his wife.

Afterwards, I gave his wife a little bottle of healing oil and told her to keep anointing him with it every day. She told me that they had been praying for his healing every day in the Garden Tomb as they explained that it was his last trip to Israel, as Ed had been struggling with his illness which was affecting his brain. Then they let me share about our friend Canon Andrew White and how struggled with MS but God uses him and sustains him on his sick bed and he continues to travel and do God's work despite his illness Ed and his wife both cried and were very emotional because they felt encouraged by Andrew's story.

We didn't get to say goodbye to Andrew before he left because he's such an incredibly busy man with a tight schedule, plus I had a bout of malaria that made me quite feverish at night time. I don't like saying goodbye anyway as

I prefer to believe that we will see each other again soon. Good bye for me is too final.

The following day was when we had to go back home to good old Blighty. We had one final look at the beautiful view of 'God's Compound' which we will miss hugely, although I did draw a picture of the view of roof tops and church domes. We were also sad when we had to say our farewells to Michael, the lovely Jewish man from England who is so inoffensive and dedicated to his faith. Therefore we left him some packet food and cleaning items, whilst at the same time we gave the hostel receptionist some Walt Disney plates and mugs for his children of which he was very grateful for.

After such an amazing experience, it was only on the plane going home that we began to realise that we were now officially married and had been blessed by God with such an incredible journey that God had planned. From the wedding given by our dear friend the Vicar of Baghdad and a beautiful wedding reception with the banquet for the

'The marriage of the Seder Lamb', 'Passover meal', thanks to Andrew White and Christine Darg. However, we have to give thanks to God, the Almighty Father, and God of all creation as you couldn't have made it up, not with Creator God, always creating. Our dear friend, Canon Andrew White, had encouraged us to walk on water and do things and go places and meet people we never thought were possible because as he says, DON'T TAKE CARE, TAKE RISKS.

Brian, Ken, Elaine and Canon Andrew White
Thank you for being obedient to God and asking me to join you on this amazing journey with Ha Shem.

Comments from Canon Andrew White,
famous Vicar of Baghdad.

Canon Andrew White wrote "The fact is that this is an incredible story that Elaine tells so well! Elaine, you were truly amazing. This was a highly important venture, one of the most important ministers in Iraq, who just happened to be the judge who tried the most famous dictator for many decades. I knew that his coming here for surgery was no little matter.

There were not least major security issues and my team was organising everything. I knew though that we needed more help. I prayed, Lord, who should this be? Within moments, God (Andrew uses G-d in this way as Jewish rabbis don't speak G-d's name) told me I would find them on Facebook. I looked, found Elaine's profile and God said, "It is her."

I did not know you or anything about you but the Lord had spoken and I responded. I have never phoned anybody before asking them to do such a monumental task before, especially when I did not know them. God knew you though and used you to do an incredible job. You loved them, cared for them and showed them the love of Jesus to them. All they could say was how much your love and care meant to them. The Minister said to me this care was not human care, it was the love and care of God. You were the chosen by God to do this work and you were simply wonderful and I thank you from the bottom of my heart. This book is indeed about taking risks. It is an incredible accurate story where I learned so much about even my own story and it is all accurate. The story of somebody who was struggling at the bottom, ends up living at the top with some of the people who hanged the history of the world. This is the incredible story of what can really happen if you take risks. Elaine did, you can also.

Andrew Paul Bartholomew White."

When I prayed, "Lord, is this all you have for my life?" within two weeks, God's reply was more than I could imagine and He used me to share the love of Jesus with a wonderful family who needed some help and support in a time of need and difficulty. This family where people who had gone through great loss, personal suffering and seen mass genocide, at the hands of an evil despot, being a well-known family in the media and worried about their safety, God came to their rescue. The God of Abraham, Isaac and Jacob, Ha Shem looked down on the family with mercy and used a man who loves Ha Shem and Yeshua the Messiah to come to their aid as help from the sanctuary. He used his child to orchestrate

His love, His kindness and mercy with two more of his children saved by the grace of Yeshua Messiah to share with them His love and His compassion. It was not by chance all of this happened, but by His power and might, the God of justice, the Lord over his people, the Lord over his nation, our God almighty for such a time as this.

God bless, Elaine Trimlett Glover

If you want salvation Ha Shem through Yeshua Messiah,
Just pray this simple prayer:
Lord, forgive me, I am a sinner.
Thank you that you took my place on the cross as an Atonement for my sin.
Thank you that you died for me and you said, "It is finished."
Thank you that you rose again on the third day.
Thank you that you are a risen living God, whose coming Back for His bride.
Lord come into my life as Lord and Saviour.
I denounce Satan, he's a lair, a robber and a murderer.
Come into give me life,
Thank you for your forgiveness and freedom in abundance.
I want to take up my cross and follow you.
There is power in the name of Yeshua and blood that He Shed to break every chain of sin and sickness.
Amen.